Windo

assis

OTHER TITLES OF INTEREST

Windows 95 assistant

by

Ian Sinclair

BERNARD BABANI (publishing) LTD

THE GRAMPIANS

SHEPHERDS BUSH ROAD

LONDON W6 7NF

ENGLAND

PLEASE NOTE

Although every care has been taken with the production of this book to ensure that any projects, designs, modifications and/or programs, etc., contained herewith, operate in a correct and safe manner and also that any components specified are normally available in Great Britain, the Publishers and Author(s) do not accept responsibility in any way for the failure (including fault in design) of any project, design, modification or program to work correctly or to cause damage to any equipment that it may be connected to or used in conjunction with, or in respect of any other damage or injury that may be so caused, nor do the Publishers accept responsibility in any way for the failure to obtain specified components.

Notice is also given that if equipment that is still under warranty is modified in any way or used or connected with home-built equipment then that warranty may be void.

© 1997 BERNARD BABANI (publishing) LTD

First Published – January 1997

British Library Cataloguing in Publication Data:

A catalogue record for this book is available from the British Library

ISBN 0 85934 421 5

Cover Design by Gregor Arthur
Cover Illustration by Adam Willis
Printed and Bound in Great Britain by Cox & Wyman Ltd, Reading

ABOUT THIS BOOK

The Windows 95 assistant is a new concept, a way of getting help whether you have the computer switched on or not. It's faster than clicking from one topic to another, and for most actions, you could have looked up your help in this book before the hard drive stops clicking on your computer on a similar mission. It has been written around Windows 95 and much of the advice will apply to later versions.

What makes this book different is its organisation. There is a short index of actions that are not listed in the main section, so that you can look up their use in the longer references. The main text consists of the most frequently needed aspects of Windows for which assistance is needed, all in alphabetical order. In this list, even the main menu items of Windows (like Start) have entries so that you can remind yourself of the most elementary points as well as of the details of actions that may be new to you, along with advice and notes that you may not have thought of. In all cases, you should look up the main word in any phrase. For example, if you want to look up *documents list*, the important word is *document* and that's what you look up in the main index.

In addition, there are notes and comments so that you can see why one method might be preferable to another, or why you might want to use some Windows 95 command that you have no experience with.

To make this book useful without being too bulky, some complications have been omitted. We assume that you *use* Windows 95 as distinct from being a programmer who is writing for Windows, so that topics like Visual Basic or macros are omitted. We assume that you want Help with Windows, not for Word, Excel or Access. We assume that you are working solo or in a small network, and that someone else can organise actions like Postboxes and Email.

What we have done is to concentrate on the assistance that is most needed. In each item dealt with, the sub-headings are not necessarily in alphabetical order, because that's not the order in which you need help. The main part of this book provides your assistance, and there is also an index of cross-references at the start of the book so that you can look up terms that are not included in the main index.

Take a look, try it for yourself. At a time when manufacturers have abandoned manuals in favour of Help files, real help is here, at hand.

Ian Sinclair, Winter 1996

ABOUT THE AUTHOR

Ian Sinclair was born in 1932 in Tayport, Fife, and graduated from the University of St. Andrews in 1956. In that year, he joined the English Electric Valve Co. in Chelmsford, Essex, to work on the design of specialised cathode-ray tubes, and later on small transmitting valves and TV transmitting tubes.

In 1966, he became an assistant lecturer at Hornchurch Technical College, and in 1967 joined the staff of Braintree College of F.E. as a lecturer. His first book, "Understanding Electronic Components" was published in 1972, and he has been writing ever since, particularly for the novice in Electronics or Computing. The interest in computing arose after seeing a Tandy TRS80 in San Francisco in 1977, and of his 180 published books, about half have been on computing topics, starting with a guide to Microsoft Basic on the TRS80 in 1979.

He left teaching in 1984 to concentrate entirely on writing, and has also gained experience in computer typesetting, particularly for mathematical texts. He has recently visited Seattle to see Microsoft at work, and to remind them that he has been using Microsoft products longer than most Microsoft employees can remember.

ACKNOWLEDGEMENTS

I would like to thank the staff of Text 100 Ltd. for providing the Windows 95 software on which this book has been based.

TRADEMARKS

ACKNOWLEDGMENTS

Cross-reference Index

Accessibility

General: Windows 95 contains a set of options that are intended to help users who find difficulties with using the default screen, mouse, sound, or keyboard systems. Some of these options, such as the sound effects when the Caps Lock key is pressed, are also useful to other users.

Selecting options: Use Start — Settings — Control Panel and when the Control Panel appears, double-click on *Accessibility Options*. This brings up a set of five panels, each with several items that can be switched on or off by clicking on a box, and each with a *Settings* button that allows you to customise the settings.

Keyboard: You can opt for *Sticky Keys* for one-finger typing, so that the Shift, Ctrl, and Alt keys can be used immediately ahead of a letter key rather than by pressing both together. The *FilterKeys* option can be turned on so that the machine will ignore either a key that is briefly stabbed or that is pressed several times in rapid succession. The *ToggleKey* action will provide a sound warning when any of the lock keys is used (Caps lock, Num lock or Scroll lock). One sound indicates that a lock key has been switched on, another sound indicates that the lock has been switched off.

Sound: *SoundSentry* will provide a visual warning when a sound is used. *ShowSound* will display a caption for speech or sound effects.

Display: You can opt for colours and fonts for easier viewing by clicking the *Use High Contrast* box.

Mouse: You can opt for *mouseless control*, using the cursor keys on the numeric keypad instead.

Other: The *AutoReset* option provides for turning off all accessibility commands after a fixed time, such as 5 minutes. *Notification* provides options for issuing warning sounds

Add/Remove programs

when features are turned on or off. Finally, you can opt for using *SerialKey* devices if you have such a (hardware) item connected.

Notes: You should try out some of these actions to find if they would be useful to you.

Add/Remove programs

General: When Windows 95 was installed on your computer, it may have used a complete installation and it will probably contain programs that you never intend to use. You can remove these unwanted files and, equally important, restore them or add others as needed, if you follow the procedure illustrated here. Programs other than the Windows 95 set can also be added or removed using the same methods.

Uninstalling W'95 files: Start Control Panel, either from Explorer or from Start — Settings. Double-click on *Add/Remove Programs* and when the panel appears click the *Windows Setup* tab. You will see a list of the sections of Windows that can be altered. These main headings are:

Accessibility Options   Accessories   Communications

Disc Tools   Microsoft Exchange   Microsoft Fax

Multi-language Support   The Microsoft Network

There is a small selection box at each title, blank if nothing in that section is used, ticked if all of the section is used. If only a selection of files is used, the box will be shaded grey and ticked. You can either add or remove a tick, or you can click the *Details* button to alter the selection of actions within a section. Click the *OK* button when you have completed your selection of details or your choices of main sections. If you are only removing files, you do not need to have the original CD-ROM or floppy discs present, but if your selection involves adding a new file, you must have the original source disc(s) in the appropriate drive.

Installing W95 files: Follow the procedure noted above, adding ticks to sections and sub-sections of the list. Make sure that the distribution CD-ROM or floppy disc 1 is in its drive before you finally click on the OK button to start installation. If you are using the floppy disc set, you will be asked to insert various discs.

Other Programs: Start *Add/Remove Programs* as above from Control Panel, and use the *Install/Uninstall* tab. To uninstall a program that is shown on the list, select it and click the *Add/Remove* button. You will be asked to confirm that you want to remove the program. TO install a program, you must have a source disc, either a floppy (the first of a set) or a CD-ROM in the appropriate drive. Click the *Install* button so that Windows will search for a program called *Install* or *Setup* on the distribution disc. Once this is found, you can click to start the installation process.

Notes: You should use **only** this system for adding or removing **Windows** files. If you remove parts of the Windows system by deleting from the Explorer view, there is a risk that you will remove files that cannot be restored by way of the *Setup* action, and you will then need to restore using the MS-DOS EXTRACT command (see the entry in this book). You can remove older programs by deleting their files, but if the name of a program appears on the *Uninstall* list it is always better to use this method of removing it.

- -

Annotating a Help topic

General: When you have used a Help item and you have found that some further explanation is needed, or that an action is capable of more than you expected, you can add a

ASCII files

note of your own to the Help item.

Method: Click the *Options* button of the Help panel (the *Edit* button if this is used in place of an *Options* button). Click *Annotate* and type your comments or notes in the small panel that appears. Click the *Save* button when you have completed your note. Other options are *Cancel*, *Delete*, *Copy* and *Paste* (so that you can copy and paste notes from one topic to another).

Notes: When a Help topic contains a note that you have added, there will be a paper-clip icon visible in the title of the help item box (not in the index, however). You can click on this icon to see the annotation.

- -

ASCII files

General: ASCII files can be read by any software that handles text, and are essential for some types of files of commands, such as AUTOEXEC.BAT or CONFIG.SYS, and for specialised purposes, such as saving or editing an exclusion dictionary for Word. In addition, an ASCII file takes up less disc space than a word-processor file. ASCII files consist of codes for the letters and punctuation marks of the alphabet, plus the numbers 0 to 9, but they are unformatted (with no fonts, bold, italics, underline or other effects).

Creating: Use the *Notepad* utility of Windows 95 to type or edit text which will be saved as an ASCII file. Notepad is limited to files of less than 64K characters, corresponding to about 8,000 words. For longer ASCII files, use the WordPad utility with the *Save As* option of *ASCII* (*Plain text*) rather than the default of *Word files*. The older *Write* utility (part of Windows 3.1) can also save files in ASCII form (called *Text files*).

4

Notes: Use ASCII format to store archive text (text for long-term backup), since this allows you to store more of your text in a limited space. See also the entries in this book for **Notepad** and **WordPad**.

- -

Associating files

General: A data file and a program can be associated, meaning that you can double-click a data file and so run the associated program with the data file loaded. For example, if any file with the TXT extension is associated with Notepad, then double-clicking a TXT file will have the effect of starting Notepad with the TXT file loaded for editing or reading. Several associations (such as TXT with Notepad) are already made for you when you install Windows 95.

Checking and creating: If you have a data file that you want to use, simply open the Explorer window to find the file and double-click on the filename. If the file already has an association made, the appropriate program will start and load the file. If no association has been made for this file type, you will see the *Open with* panel appear. You can type a brief description of the file (such as *AutoSketch drawing*), and then select a program from the list that appears. The option of *Always use this program to open this file* is ticked by default, so that double-clicking any file with the same extension letters will, in future, cause the same program to start. Click on the *OK* button when you have selected a file, but if you do not see the appropriate program in the list, click the *Options* button to see a full list of all programs on your disc.

Changing association: View your files using Explorer or My Computer. Click the *View* menu and then *Options*. When the *Options* panel appears, click the *File Types* tab to see the list of programs for which associations exist. Click on the file

Attributes of files

type whose association you want to change – you will be reminded of the current settings in the *File Type Detail* box. Click the *Edit* button. You can now alter the association.

The *Change Icon* button allows you to select another icon (for the data file) from a list. You can also alter the *Description of Type* text. The *Actions* box contains a list of actions that can be used on the data file, usually *open* and *print*. Click on *Open* and then click the *Edit* button. Click the *Browse* button to see a tree of all folders and files so that you can select the program that you want to associate with this data file type.

Options: The *New* button on the *Edit Association* panel allows you to specify another action (other than the default *open* and *print*). You need to know what actions are possible; these depend on the type of file you are associating. The *Remove* button allows you to remove an association, so that double-clicking the data file name will not automatically start a program (though you will see the *Association* panel inviting you to select a suitable program).

Notes: Association is possible only if you have a suitable program on your hard drive, so that if you have imported a file from another computer you may not be able to associate it with any program on your own hard drive. See also the entry for **File types**.

....

Attributes of files

General: All files can be 'marked' with codes that are used to allow Windows 95 and MS-DOS to distinguish the files as belonging to four classes, and these codes are called attributes. A file can have no attributes, or any combination of the four. The four main file attributes are named *archive*, *hidden*, *read-only* and *system*, and of these the *archive* and *read-only* may sometimes need to be altered. The system and hidden attributes are set on for important files and should never be altered. Setting a file as *read-only* prevents editing, and the file can only be viewed, copied, or printed until this attribute is switched off. Setting a file as *archive* allows it to be backed up by any utility that recognises this attribute – the archive code is set when a file has been altered since the last time it was backed up and reset (switched off) when a backup is made.

Change attributes: Use an *Explorer* or *My Computer* display to find the file, and click the file name. Now click *File* and *Properties* from the menu. The attributes appear as a set of four boxes at the bottom of the *Properties* panel. Usually the archive box is ticked but the others are not – the system attribute box is usually greyed out. You would normally want to use this action to set a file as read-only or to clear the read-only attribute to allow editing.

Notes: Some programs (such as Word) allow you to set the read-only attribute directly for a file. The archive bits are sometimes referred to as R–A–S–H, using the initial letters of read-only, archive, system and hidden.

• You can opt to see, in an Explorer display, files that are normally hidden. See the entry for **System files**.

• The archive attribute is not reset when you make a copy to a floppy, only when a backup system is used, such as Backup in Windows, or XCOPY in MS-DOS.

Autoexec.bat file

General: The AUTOEXEC.BAT file consists of an ASCII text file containing a set of MS-DOS commands that are executed before Windows 95 is loaded, and you should not,

Available disc space

in normal circumstances, need to edit this file. Its purpose is to set up the computer, particularly for running MS-DOS programs or for additions (such as sound cards) that were installed before Windows 95. If your computer was in use before Windows 95 was installed (using Windows 3.1 or DOS) then several portions of the file will have been modified by the installation program for Windows 95.

Editing: Start Notepad and use the Open command to look for *All files* (*.*). Look in the C:\ root folder and double-click AUTOEXEC.BAT. The file can then be edited. See *BP341 MS-DOS 6 explained* for details of how to use this file.

Bypassing: If a command in the AUTOEXEC.BAT file is causing problems with Windows 95, you can start the computer in such a way as to bypass commands. Restart the computer by using Start — Shut Down, and when the *Starting Windows 95* message appears, press and release the F8 key. From the menu that appears, select *Step by Step Confirmation*. This allows you to accept or reject each step in the setup, starting with the commands of the CONFIG.SYS file (see entry for **CONFIG.SYS**). The final step should be the AUTOEXEC.BAT file (or *Startup Command File*, as it is referred to). If you do not use this file, you can avoid starting Windows 95 and the machine will be running DOS.

Notes: If you have never used DOS, and particularly if your computer was installed with Windows 95 when you bought it, you should never need to edit AUTOEXEC.BAT or CONFIG.SYS, and you should certainly not do so unless you understand the effects that changes in these files could cause.

....

Available disc space

General: If you have a large hard drive which is less than half filled, you hardly need worry about disc space. If, however, you are using a hard drive of inadequate size, and particularly if you are using file compression (see the entry for **DriveSpace**) then you need to check available disc space at intervals. You may also want to check the available space on a floppy disc.

Methods: The simplest check is available in the *Explorer* window when the drive (hard or floppy) is selected. The available disc space is printed at the foot of the *Explorer* window, along with the space taken up by files in the selected folder.

Another option is to use *My Computer*, click the drive icon for the drive, and then click File — Properties. This brings up a pie chart which will show the relative sizes of used and unused space.

Notes: If you use DriveSpaced files, the figure for unused space may be optimistic, and you should not attempt to fill all of this space. You can use the *Compression Agent* of *Microsoft Plus!* to determine how tightly different file types are packed so as to determine for your own purposes what balance of disc speed and packing of files you want to use.

- -

Backing up files

General: You should keep backup copies of all files other than temporary files. Programs that have been installed from CD-ROM need not be backed up, because the CD-ROM format is more secure than the conventional magnetic disc. You may also feel that programs that have been supplied on floppies and installed on the hard drive need no further backup. The most important backups, then, are the data files which you generate for yourself and which cannot be replaced if they are wiped, either from carelessness or by hard drive failure.

Backup

Backup type: Backup can be in plain form, copying the file to a floppy or to a tape, or in compressed form, using either floppy or tape. For the use of the Backup command, see the entry for **Backup**.

Simple backup: You can back up files on to floppies by using a *Copy* action, provided that no single file is larger than the capacity of a floppy. You can use DriveSpace with the tightest possible compression for your floppy discs to achieve an equivalent capacity of 3 Mbyte or more on each floppy. To make the backup, place a floppy in the drive, and select the files in Explorer. Drag the files to the floppy drive icon and wait for the backup action to be completed. If the number of files requires more than one floppy you will be advised when to change discs.

Notes: The advantage of simple backup is that the files can be read by other users, and are immediately available without the need to start the more elaborate Backup program.

....

Backup

General: Backup is one of the *System Tools* set of Windows 95. It allows you to backup data in compressed form on floppies, tapes, other computers on a network, or removable hard drives. You can also use it to compare a backup file with the original, and to retrieve files from backed-up form. The process is automatic once started, though if you use floppies you may need to change discs at intervals – about 4 Mbyte can be saved on each floppy. Only a few types of tape drive (such as the Colorado Jumbo) are recognised by *Backup*, and if you use other types you will need to use the software that comes with the backup system.

Starting: Click the *Start* button, followed by *Programs*,

Backup

Accessories and *System Tools*. From the *System Tools* set, click *Backup*. The main *Microsoft Backup* panel will appear.

Selecting files for backup: Backup shows a list of folders and files in Explorer format, with a small box next to each name. Click this box to place a tick into it and so select it. Selecting a drive will select all folders and files on that drive. Selecting a folder name will select for backup all the files in that folder. You can also select file names individually. If a large number of files is selected the process can take several minutes.

Making the backup: When files have been selected, you can click the *Next Step* button. This selects a destination for the backup, and the two most likely are **floppy drive** or (if you have a tape backup) **tape**. Make sure that a blank floppy or tape is inserted into the drive, and then click the *Start Backup* button. You will be asked to type a filename for your backup, and a useful type of filename is the date (such as 8JUN96) along with an indication of the contents (DATA, SYSTEM, PROGS, etc.). When you have done this the backup will start. If you are using floppies you will be prompted to change discs at intervals. You should label these floppies in sequence, as they will need to be inserted in the same order when you restore the contents.

File set: If you are likely to back up the same selection several times, you can save it as a file set. This is particularly useful if you have selected several folders, because if the contents of the folders change, they will still be automatically selected for backup because the folder has been selected. The File set can be saved after you have selected a destination for the backup by clicking File — Save As in the menu, and providing a filename for the selection. This is saved as a file of type SET and can be obtained subsequently by using File — Open File Set the next time you make a backup.

Backup

Full System Backup: A file set for *Full System Backup* (FSB) is provided and can be loaded in when you are asked to select files. An FSB will backup all of the files on the hard drive, including the important Windows registry files, so that you should make at least one backup of this type if you have a tape drive or a removable hard drive (the size of the FSB makes it unlikely that you will want to use floppies for this purpose). You can decrease the size of the FSB set by removing from it all data files and, if necessary, all program files other than the Windows set. You will be asked to confirm any change to the FSB set.

Options: The Settings — Options menu allows you to specify options for general use and for the three main actions of Backup, Restore and Compare. These are detailed below:

General: The options boxes provide for turning on audible prompts and for overwriting old status log files. Both of these can normally be ticked, unless there is some particular reason for retaining old log files.

Backup. The main option box is labelled *Quit Backup after operation is finished*, and this can be ticked if you want to resume normal working as soon as possible after making a backup. You can also choose between making a full backup on all selected files and making an incremental backup only of files that have changed since the last full backup. See later for details of incremental backup.

The *Advanced* section has four option boxes. The *Verify backup* data box will automatically carry out a file comparison between the backup copy and the original and report on any differences. The box labelled *Use Data Compression* should be ticked, particularly if you are backing up to floppies, as it makes full use of the available storage space. The option to *Format if necessary on tape backup* provides for using unformatted tape. The option of

12

Always erase on tape backup allows the same tape to be used over and over again for a full backup, and must not be used if you want to make incremental backups on the same tape. The last option is *Always erase on floppy disc backup*, and this also is usually desirable unless you want to avoid the possibility of wiping a disc by mistake.

Restore. As for Backup, the main option is the *Quit Restore after operation is finished*, and you will probably want to tick this option. You can also choose whether to restore backup files to the *Original location* (the default), to an *alternative location*, or to an *alternative location, into a single folder (directory)*. The use of an alternative location allows you, for example, to place all of your files on a new hard drive (added in parallel with the original), and the use of a single folder allows a set of files to be restored from a backup so that you can find them all without having to search through a set of folders.

The *Advanced* section provides for verifying restored data against the backup copy, and the options for files of the same name are *Never overwrite files*, *Overwrite older files only*, or *Overwrite files*. If you use this last option you can opt for a prompt message each time a file is to be overwritten.

Compare. The *Quit after operation is finished* option is used in this set also. The file comparison options are *Original location*, *Alternate location*, and *Alternate location, single folder (directory)*.

The other options provide for Drag and Drop and for File Filtering. The Drag and Drop options allow you to specify how you want Backup to proceed when you have the Backup program displayed as an icon and you have selected files and dragged them to the Backup icon. The options are to *Run Backup Minimized*, to *Confirm Operation before Beginning*, and to *Quit after Backup is Completed*. *File filtering* allows

Backup

you to specify file types (in the form of extension letters) that you want to exclude from a backup, or to exclude files on the basis of date.

Incremental backup: You can opt for full or incremental backup of the files you have selected. A *Full backup*, as the name suggests, backs up the files completely, so that they can be restored to the state they were in at the time of the backup. An *Incremental backup* can be made only following a full backup of the same files, and it backs up only the changes in files. This action should be reserved for specialised purposes, because it does not back up new files that have been added to folders, only changes in files that were previously backed up. You must clear the *Always Erase on Tape Backup* option box before you add an incremental backup to a tape that contains an existing full backup. When you recover files, both the full backup and the incremental backup must be present.

Notes: The Backup software is essentially the same as is provided for the Colorado Jumbo tape backup system (a Hewlett-Packard product), but the Colorado software also allows for restoring the contents of a hard drive after a catastrophic failure which has required replacement of the drive. This uses a System (Startup) floppy disc with the Colorado software on it. There is no provision for this action in the Microsoft Backup version, but if you use the Colorado drive, you can prepare floppies for this type of emergency, but use Microsoft Backup for your normal backup actions.

• The types of tape drive supported in Windows 95 are of the built-in QIC 40, 80 and 3010 type, manufactured by Colorado, Conner, Iomega or Wangtek; or the externally connected parallel-port QIC types manufactured by Colorado. Other drives are not recognised, and must use their own software – this applies to the popular Travan type of drive.

- The log files for backup are called *Error.log* and are located in the Program Files — Accessories — Log folder, normally on the C:\ drive.

....

Battery actions

General: Modern laptop computers are not noted for long battery life, and Windows 95 contains utilities that assist in monitoring the state of the battery and reducing the drain on the battery. Several such items are usually built into the hardware, such as running the hard drive only when necessary, dimming the display, and shutting off other actions when not in use. The battery extending actions in Windows 95 assume the use of modern hardware, such as Advanced Power Management (*APM 1.1*) or the VESA BIOS extensions for power management (*VBE/PM*). No battery-saving options will appear if the hardware of your computer does not support them.

Monitor: Click *Start*, followed by *Settings* and *Control Panel*, and from Control Panel double-click *Display*. For suitable hardware, there will be a box labelled *Low-power Standby* which you can tick so that the monitor will be switched off after a set time of inactivity – you can select this time, usually five or ten minutes, in the *Minutes* box. The *Shut Off Monitor* box can also be ticked (specifying a longer time than the *Standby* period).

Battery meter: If your hardware has been correctly installed, there will be an icon on the Taskbar for checking battery condition – this can be an image of a battery or a (US-type) electric plug. Point to this icon to find what percentage of a full charge is available to you, or double-click for more information on battery state. If no Power icon appears on the

Briefcase

Taskbar, click the *Power Properties* icon in Control Panel – this will appear only if the hardware supports these features.

Note: Use a car or mains adapter as far as is possible for supplying your portable so as to reduce the drain on the internal batteries.

Briefcase

General: Briefcase is a facility aimed at anyone who uses a portable machine working on files that are copied from a desktop machine in the office. With the machines connected (by direct cable or over a network), you can drag files from the main computer to the Briefcase icon on the portable computer, and use these files when the machines are disconnected. When you reconnect, clicking the option of *Update All in Briefcase* will automatically update all the affected files in the desktop computer so that they are identical to the altered version in the portable machine. Briefcase is available only if you selected the *Portable* option when Windows 95 was installed on the portable machine (or if you performed a *Custom* installation and specified *Briefcase*). If your portable machine does not show the Briefcase icon on its Desktop display, you can repeat the *Install* action to install just this one component.

Checking files: Using the Briefcase folder, click the file(s) you want to check. Click File — Properties and click the *Update Status* tab. If you are connected to the main computer, you can click *Find Original* to get the file whose copy is in the portable machine. You can check all of the Briefcase files (and folders) from the View — Details menu, reading the *Status* report for each file that appears.

Using a floppy: Files can be updated even if there is no cable or network connection between the desktop machine and the portable, but the set of actions is more complicated. The desktop machine must have used the *Portable* setup option so that the *My Briefcase* icon appears on the Desktop (use Setup if necessary to install this icon). With a floppy in the drive of the desktop machine, drag files/folders to the *My Briefcase* icon on the desktop. Drag the Briefcase to the floppy drive symbol to copy the files to the floppy. Remove the floppy from the desktop computer and insert it into the portable. Copy the files and edit them in the portable, copying back to the floppy when completed. Back in the office, put the floppy into its drive in the desktop machine and double-click the *My Briefcase* icon on the desktop. Click the *Update All* item in the Briefcase menu. If you want to select files for updating, make the selection and click *Update Selection*.

Orphans: An orphan is a file that has been split from the original (on the main computer), so that it belongs entirely with the portable machine and cannot be used to update the corresponding file on the main machine (except by copying it to the main machine). To create an orphan, click the file and click the *Split from Original* menu item.

Notes: The Briefcase action is also referred to as *synchronising files*.

....

Calculator

General: The Calculator utility of Windows 95 can be used as an on-screen simple arithmetical calculator, or as a full scientific calculator. The advantage, as compared to a hand-held calculator, is that the input and output numbers can be cut and pasted to and from other Windows 95 programs and documents.

Launching: Start Calculator by clicking on its icon in the Start — Programs — Accessories menu. If Calculator is not

Calculator

in the Start menu, find the file by using Explorer, and double-click on the name. You can use the Settings — Taskbar option of the Start menu to place the Calculator icon and shortcut into the Accessories set. The Calculator window **cannot** be re-sized, but it can be moved. You can use the calculator either by clicking on the displayed keys, or using equivalent keyboard keys (see later for the list of keys for items other than numbers or simple arithmetic).

Display: The Calculator display can be toggled between *Standard* and *Scientific* (click in the View menu). The *Standard* calculator has the key arrangement of an ordinary pocket calculator with square root, percentage and inverse (1/x) keys, along with the usual memory keys MC, MR, MS and M+, meaning memory clear, memory recall, memory store and memory add, respectively. The *Back* key, not generally available on a pocket calculator, will strip digits from a number starting from the right hand side, and is used to reduce the number of decimal places.

The *Scientific* calculator uses an extended keyboard (though without the square root key) to provide a full set of scientific and statistical functions. The use of these functions is beyond the scope of this book and, in general, if you need the *Scientific* Calculator you will have had experience of using these functions on a pocket calculator.

Cut and Paste: You can type a calculation in Notepad, *Copy* and *Paste* it to Calculator, and then *Copy* and *Paste* the result back to Notepad. You must enter the calculation in correct format into Notepad (for example. **4.75*3.14=** to multiply these numbers, or **5.7*4.5=@** to multiply and then take a square root on the *Standard* calculator), and a list follows of the key equivalents that can be used on the Calculator and in Notepad typing.

Key equivalents of buttons: The following list applies to the

Scientific calculator, but apart from square root and percentage, the *Standard* calculator uses the same keys for the same buttons. The @ key is used for square root on the *Standard* calculator, which also uses the % key for percentages.

Button	Key	Button	Key	Button	Key	Button	Key
%	%	Back	BACK	Hyp	h	Pi	p
(	(	Bin	F8	Ln	n	Rad	F3
)	)	Byte	F4	Int	;	s	Ctrl-d
*	*	C	Esc	Inv	I	Sin	s
+	+	CE	Del	log	l	inv x^2	I@
+/–	F9	Cos	o	Lsh	<	Sta	Ctrl-s
–	–	Dat	Ins	M+	Ctrl-p	Sum	Ctrl-t
.	. or,	Dec	F6	MC	Ctrl-l	Tan	t
/	/	Deg	F2	Mod	%	Word	F3
dms	m	MR	Ctrl-r	Xor	^	1/x	r
Dword	F2	MS	Ctrl-m	x^2	@	=	Enter
Exp	x	n!	!	x^3	#	F-E	v
Not	~	x^y	y	And	&	Grad	F4
Oct	F7	Ave	Ctrl-a	Hex	F5	Or	|

Notes: All results on the Standard calculator are printed to 11 places of decimals – use the *Back* button to reduce the number of decimal places.

. . . .

Capturing screen

General: Any complete screen or window can be captured to the Clipboard by using the *Print Screen* key. The Clipboard image can then be loaded into any bitmap editor, such as Paint, to be saved, edited and printed as required.

Cascading/tiling windows

Action: Pressing the *Print Screen* key by itself will copy the entire screen display to the Clipboard. Using the *Alt* key along with the *Print Screen* key will capture the current Window, if more than one window is being displayed.

Using an image: A captured image can be pasted directly into a Word document, using the Edit — Paste command, or by the same method into Paint/tiling or any other bitmap package.

Notes: Working with screen images is faster and easier if the standard VGA 640 × 480, 16-colour screen is used. The captured images from screens that use higher resolution and/or larger numbers of colours are very much larger and need a fast processor to work with.

. . . .

Cascading/tiling windows

General: When several windows are in use, they can be *cascaded* or *tiled*. Cascaded windows overlap, with one window shown entirely and the header bars of the others visibly stacked behind it. Tiled windows are arranged so that the whole of each window can be seen, with each window in a reduced size. Tiling can be horizontal (each window is a horizontal strip) or vertical (each window is a vertical strip).

Cascading: The windows must be open and not minimised. Click any blank portion of the Taskbar using the right-hand mouse button. From the menu that appears, click *Cascade* if you want to cascade the windows, otherwise select *Tile Horizontally* or *Tile Vertically*.

Restoring windows: You can close the cascaded or tiled windows that you do not need by clicking on the close icon (X symbol) at the top right hand corner of the header bar. If you want to restore the windows to their original state, click again on a blank portion of the Taskbar using the right-hand mouse button, and from the menu select *Undo Cascade/Tile*.

Notes: If you are using a Help screen, it will remain on top rather than being cascaded if you have opted for the (default) *Help on Top* option.

CD Player

General: CD Player allows you to play your CD recordings on a computer that is equipped with a CD-ROM drive, a sound card, and loudspeakers (or earphones). You can opt for *AutoPlay*, so that a CD will start to play whenever you insert the disc in the drive.

Autoplay: To set AutoPlay, open Explorer and then click View — Options — File Types. Find the *Type* called *AudioCD* and click the *Edit* button. The word *Play* should appear in the *Actions* list. Click on this word and then click the *Set Default* button.

If the word *Play* is **not** on the *Actions* list, click the *Edit* button. on the panel that appears, and click in the *Actions* panel. Type the word *Play*, and then move to the *Application used to perform this action* panel. Use the Browse key to find the program CDPLAYER.EXE (usually in the C:\WINDOWS folder), and click. When this panel is complete, click on *Play* and *Set Default* as noted above.

- You can remove the AutoPlay action from the same menu by clicking on *Play* and then on the *Remove* button.

- You can also temporarily disable the AutoPlay action if you hold down the Shift key when you load in an audio CD.

Using CD Player: The CD Player panel provides information on the audio CD that has been inserted, with a

CD Player

large (but not bright) display of time, and strips for *Artist*, *Title*, and *Track*. If no disc has been inserted the *Artist* text will read: *Data or no disc loaded*, meaning that you have either inserted no disc or that you have used a CD-ROM with no music content. If no disc has been inserted, the *Title* bar will read: *Please insert an audio compact disc*.

The icons next to the time display are the usual (video recorder style) play, pause, stop, previous track, skip backwards, skip forwards, next track, and eject actions.

The icons above the timer panel are for *Edit play list*, *Show elapsed track time*, *Show remaining track time*, *Show remaining disc time*, *Play tracks at random*, *Continuous play*, and *Play start of each track* respectively. These items are also available from the *Disc*, *View* and *Options* menus.

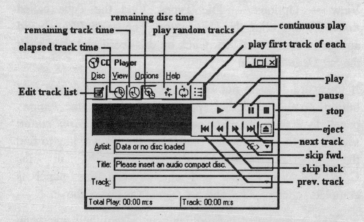

Editing Play list data: Currently, music CDs do not contain track data, but you can enter such data into a file on the hard drive that will be loaded when your CD is identified. This is done through the *Play list* when an audio disc has been loaded. When you click on the icon or the menu item, you will see a panel that contains lines marked *Drive*, *Artist* and *Title*, and you can enter your own text into the *Artist* and

CD-ROM drive

Title lines. Below these is space for the *Play List* and *Available Tracks*, used for display only. You can enter information for each track on the bottom line which will initially be marked as *Track 01*. When you have typed data, click the Set *Name* key to add the information to the *Play List* and *Available Tracks* list.

Making a Play List: The default *Play List* consists of all tracks in sequence. You can select a track by clicking in the *Play List* and remove it by clicking on the *Remove* button, and you can add a track by clicking on a name in the *Available Tracks* list and clicking on the *Add* button. In this way, you can make up a play list of your own, and you can add a track more than once. If necessary, you can delete the entire *Play* list by clicking on the *Clear All* button. You can replace all tracks in the *Play List* (using the *Available Tracks* list) by clicking the *Reset* button. You can also alter the order of tracks in the *Play List* by dragging track titles from one position to another.

Options: The Options —Preferences menu item allows you to select each of the following: *Stop CD Player on Exit*, *Save Settings on Exit* and *Show Tool Tips*. You can also change the default time of 15 seconds gap between tracks.

Notes: See also the entries for **Volume control, Media Player**.

CD-ROM drive

General: If a CD-ROM drive was installed in your computer before Windows 95 was installed, the CD-ROM drive will have been detected and correctly installed into the Windows system. If you install a modern CD-ROM drive *after* having installed Windows 95 you should allow Windows to detect the drive rather than using the processes (such as altering the

23

CD-ROM drive

CONFIG.SYS file) that were used for installation using DOS or Windows 3.1.

Installation: If you need to install a new CD-ROM drive to run under Windows 95, make certain that the hardware part of the installation (locating drive, connecting cables) is correctly carried out with the power off. Start the computer and then shut down any programs other than Explorer. Click the Start button and then Settings — Control Panel. Alternatively, if you are running Explorer, click the Control Panel item in the Explorer list. Double-click the *Add New Hardware* item, and start the Wizard running. Opt to allow Windows to find the new hardware (this is more likely to ensure correct installation) and when the searching process starts, wait until the action is completed. When the Wizard is finished, the CD-ROM drive should be correctly installed.

Configuring: When a CD-ROM drive has been installed, you need to configure it for the performance you want. If you are using it in conjunction with a sound card and loudspeakers, you may want to use *AutoPlay*, so that inserting an audio CD will start that disc playing. See the **CD Player** entry for details. The other configuration action is to make the best possible use of the drive you have installed. Drives are classed as double-speed, quad-speed, hex-speed and so on (single-speed is now very rare), and this needs to be recognised by Windows. Click on Start — Settings — Control Panel or click on the Control Panel item of Explorer. Double-click on System — Performance — File System — CD ROM to see the CD ROM performance panel. Look for the *Access Pattern* box, and click the arrowhead to see the list of drive speeds. Click on the drive speed (such as *Quad-speed*) that you are using. You may also want to increase the size of memory cache that the drive uses, since this also will aid fast access to data. To do this, drag the arrow indicator on the *Supplemental Cache Size* indicator closer towards the

Large side (right hand side). If you have a large memory size (16 Mbyte or more) you can drag the slider all the way to the *Large* side.

Device settings: You should also check device settings. Start the Control Panel — System from the *Start* button or the Explorer, and select the *Device Manager* tab. On this list of devices, click on *CD-ROM* and then double-click on the name of the drive that appears. On the two-tab panel that appears, click on *Settings*. The *Options* in this panel are normally made for you by Windows when the drive is installed, but you might want to make certain that the *Auto Insert Notification* is ticked. You can also check the drive letter and, if necessary, change it (unless this portion is greyed out). You can also specify a range of letters to be reserved for the CD-ROM drive.

- Users of SCSI drives should check that the other options are also ticked, and the *Disconnect* option is set for IDE and EIDE drive connections.

Using CD-ROM: You will normally use CD-ROM for program installation or as a data source for an installed program. When you need to install a program, insert the CD disc and double-click the *Add/Remove Programs* item in the Control Panel. Follow the Wizard instructions, but if the CD-ROM is not recognised you can use the *Browse* action to locate the CD-ROM drive letter and find the INSTALL or SETUP program for the new software.

- When you need to use the CD for data, running its associated program (such as Encarta, for example) will automatically make use of the CD.

Notes: If you have installed programs that use the CD as a data source and you subsequently change the CD-ROM drive letter you may need to re-install the programs, as they will try to use the old drive letter. For example, if your CD-ROM drive used the letter D, and you subsequently install a new hard drive, this will force the CD-ROM drive to use the letter E (or higher, if the new hard drive is partitioned), and this new letter will not necessarily be recognised by some of your existing software.

- Even if a program makes considerable use of a CD-ROM for data, it will usually require space on the hard drive. For example, Encarta requires some 6 Mbyte of hard drive space.

Character map

General: The Character map is used to insert symbols and foreign characters into text and is available for use by programs that run under Windows 95. For example, Word-7 can use the Character map by way of its Insert — Symbol menu. For other programs such as Notepad, you can call up the Character Map display.

Launching: If Character Map was installed with Windows, 95 you can launch it by using Start — Programs — Accessories and clicking on *Character Map*. You can make a shortcut to this if you often use the Character Map, and one ready-made shortcut exists in the Help menu for Character Map. If Character Map is not present in your system, you can use Windows 95 Setup and specify that you want to install this program only, see the entry for **Installing Windows 95 components.**

Using: Select from the *Font* list the font set from which you want to take special characters. This will usually be the font you are currently using if you want to add accented characters, or the *Symbol* or *Wingdings* fonts for Greek, mathematical and other symbols. Use *System* or *Terminal* fonts if you want to match the use of these fonts in graphics programs.

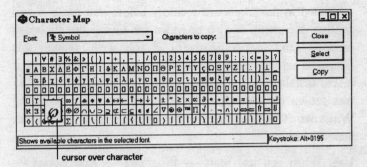

cursor over character

With the correct font in use, double-click on the character you want to add, or single-click on the character and then click on the *Select* button.. You can see that character magnified if you hold down the mouse button before double-clicking. Each double-clicked character will appear in the *Characters to copy* space and you can place a number of consecutive characters into this space. Click the *Copy* button when you are ready, and then switch back to the document that you are working on. Place the cursor and click in the position where you want the character to appear, then click Edit — Paste. If the characters change when you *Paste* them in, select them, and then change to the font that you used in the Character Map. If your subsequent typing makes use of characters that are not on your keyboard, select them and change back to your original font.

Notes: Character Map cannot be used on programs that run under DOS. If you are using Word-7, the method of inserting characters makes use of the Character Map display, but is simpler – the character is inserted automatically with no need to use the *Copy* and *Paste* actions.

Clipboard Viewer

Clipboard Viewer

General: The Clipboard Viewer allows you to see what is contained in the Clipboard memory before you paste it into another document. It also provides for saving the clipboard contents (and re-loading them) if you wish, though this facility is seldom used. Clipboard Viewer is available only if it was installed as one of the Accessories when Windows 95 was set up on your computer. See the entry for **Installing Windows 95 components** for adding this and other accessories.

Use: When you use Start — Programs — Accessories — Clipboard Viewer you will see the Clipboard Viewer panel appear as a small window which can be moved and/or re-sized as required. If anything has been captured to the Clipboard, it will appear in the *Viewer* panel.

Save and Open: Any information in the Clipboard can be saved by using the File — Save As option. This will save the information as a CLP file which can later be opened from Clipboard. This facility is seldom needed, because most captured images are pasted into other documents and saved as part of such documents.

File Conversion: Information in the Clipboard can be converted to another format, and the permitted formats depend on whether text or graphics is being used. Click the *Display* menu heading to see the permitted formats.

Notes: Clipboard Viewer is of little use if you use the Clipboard predominantly as an intermediate in Cut and Paste actions and unless you find the *Save As* or the *Conversion* options useful you need not install the Clipboard Viewer.

Clock

General: The Clock utility of Windows 95 provides a time display on the Taskbar, unlike the window display of the clock in Windows 3.1. The Taskbar clock icon can also provide date information.

Setting up: Click Start — Settings — Taskbar and in the *Taskbar Options* panel, click the selection box marked *Show Clock*. This will ensure that the time display appears in the Taskbar.

Use: You can read the time from the Taskbar display, and if you hold the pointer on this display, the date will appear also.

Options: Click the time display on the Taskbar, using the right-hand mouse button. You can then select *Adjust Date/Time* from the menu. Alternatively, double-click the time display using the left-hand mouse button. You can also adjust the *Time Zone* from this display.

Notes: The Date/Time and Time Zone can also be changed from the Control Panel — Date/Time option.

Colours

General: The number of colours that you can use depends on what range your monitor will permit, and on the speed you want to achieve on your computer. Using the standard 16-colour and 640 × 480 resolution display on the monitor ensures that programs which make use of screen images will run as fast as possible. For better appearance of pictures you may want to use the higher options for colours, such as *256*, *High Colour* (65536 colours) or *True Colour* (16 million colours, for photographic quality), but using these options will noticeably slow down your work unless you are using a very fast machine with a graphics accelerator card that

Colours

contains a generous amount of memory, typically 2 Mbyte. In addition, images in *True Colour* will demand a very large amount of hard drive and memory space.

Colour settings: Save data and close down all programs except Explorer. Click Start — Settings — Control Panel, or click Control Panel from the Explorer display. Double-click on the *Display* icon and then select the *Settings* tab. On this panel, select the *Colour Palette* setting that you want from the set that appears when you click the arrowhead. When you click the *OK* button you will be notified that you must restart the computer for the new settings to take effect. Remember that the higher settings such as *High Colour* and *True Colour* can be used only if your monitor supports them.

* The resolution settings for the monitor can also be changed in this panel by dragging the Desktop Area slider to one of the other settings. The standard settings are 640 × 480, 800 × 600 and 1024 × 768. As for colours, the higher settings are available only if your monitor supports them.

Colour scheme: You can select the colours that are used for different parts of the Windows display. Use the Control Panel Display option as above and click the *Appearance* tab. This opens a panel that displays the appearance of a typical window. You can click on any part of this display to see the name appear in the *Item* panel, along with entries in the *Size* and *Colour* boxes. This allows you to change the size, colour and font used for any part of a typical window display.

You can select from a range of preset displays. These are named, but the names are not necessarily a useful guide to their appearance. The current set of names is as follows, using abbreviation HC for High Contrast, L for Large and EL for Extra Large.

Colours

Brick   Desert   Eggplant   HC Black   HC Black (EL)

HC Black (L)   HC White   HC White (EL)

HC White (L)   Lilac   Lilac (L)   Maple

Marine (High colour)   Plum (High colour) (M)

Pumpkin (L)   Rainy Day   Red, White & Blue (VGA)

Rose   Rose (L)   Slate   Spruce   Stars & Stripes (VGA)

Storm (VGA)   Teal (VGA)   Wheat   Windows Standard

Windows Standard (EL)   Windows Standard (L)

- The larger sizes are useful when you are using the higher screen resolution figures.

You can create your own set of colours by selecting a colour for each portion of the display from the *Item* set, and assigning a colour from the list. The number of colours that you can select from depends on which colour options (16, 256, etc.) that you have set in the *Colour Palette*, and includes some grey or shaded options. Having created a display in this way, you can save it using a filename of your own by clicking the *Save As* button. If you use a name with no capital letters you can distinguish your own colour sets from these supplied with Windows.

The standard portions of a window are:

3-D Objects   Active Title Bar   Active Window Border

Application Background   Caption Buttons   Desktop

Icon   Icon Spacing (Horizontal)   Icon Spacing (Vertical)

Inactive Title Bar   Inactive Window Border   Menu

Message Bar   Palette Title   Scrollbar

Selected Items   Tooltips   Window

Compressed drives

- Remember that you can also change the fonts that are used for each portion of a Window display. The standard font is the MS Sans Serif, but you may prefer the appearance of some of the other fonts that you have on your hard drive.

Note: If you are using screen-grabs to illustrate a document, it's often better to use a set of grey shades or colours that provide good contrast, particularly if the document will be printed on a monochrome printer.

- These colour schemes are used only for Windows programs, and will not appear in MS-DOS programs that you run using Windows 95.

....

Compressed drives

General: A hard or floppy drive normally stores data using a version of the same codes as are used in the memory. It is possible to reduce the amount of drive space that is required by **compressing** the data, eliminating repetition and making more efficient use of the way that the disc is organised. Windows 95 does this using DriveSpace-2, and more efficient compression methods are use in DriveSpace-3, part of the Microsoft Plus! option that was made available at the same time as Windows 95. The Backup utility also uses a very efficient packing system.

- The compression action on a hard drive creates an additional drive letter, often H. This drive, called the Host, is the real physical drive, which contains just one large file (called the CVF, compressed volume file), which can be as large as the full capacity of the drive. This CVF will have a filename which is typically DRVSPACE.000. The normal drive letter C: now applies to files that are packed into this CVF.

32

Compressed drives

Do You Need It? If your hard drive is inadequate, the best solution is to fit a much larger (which does not mean physically larger) drive. Drives of 1 Gbyte or more are now available at reasonable prices. If this is impossible, the use of drive compression allows you to continuing to use the existing drive to store a much larger amount of data and programs.

• You must always ensure that you have adequate backups of your files before you opt to compress your hard drive, and this applies also if you are performing the opposite action of decompressing (after you have added another hard drive to increase the total capacity).

Compressing a Drive: Click Start — Programs — Accessories — System Tools — DriveSpace to start the program. When the *DriveSpace* panel appears, it will show a list of existing drives, and you can click on the hard drive C: (or on a floppy drive if there is a floppy disc in that drive). Now click the *Drive* menu, and the *Compress* option to see a diagram showing what improvements in space can be obtained by using compression. The options in this panel are to select a drive letter for the *Host*, or to specify how much of the host should not be compressed. Unless you know what you are doing, it's better to ignore the options and allow the default values to be used.

Compression is a lengthy process for a hard drive, and for an original capacity of 250 Mbyte or more you need to allow several hours for compression, particularly if the drive was almost full in its uncompressed state. When the process is completed you will see another display that shows the new amount of free space and used space on the CVF. Typically, you may find that a 250 Mbyte hard drive now appears to have a total capacity of 416 Mbyte. The display also shows the assumed compression ratio (such as 2.0:1) and the actual

Compressed drives

compression ratio (such as 1.8:1).

- If you have installed Microsoft Plus!, the name *Compression Agent* will appear rather than *DriveSpace*.

Maintenance: A compressed drive can be maintained using the normal disc utilities such as ScanDisk and Disc Defragmenter. You can also use the DriveSpace program itself to adjust the free space on a disc. For **experienced PC users only**, you can leave enough uncompressed space on a drive to hold the Windows swap file. The default arrangement is to use the compressed file to hold the Windows swap file (WIN386.SWP), but this slows down the action of swapping between memory and this file. Creating a permanent swap file and storing it on an uncompressed portion of the hard drive (as was done on Windows 3.1) makes for faster swapping.

Floppies: If you want to use compressed floppies along with uncompressed floppies, you can compress any floppy disc using the normal procedure outlined above. You should also opt for *Automounting*, meaning that when a compressed floppy is placed in the drive it will be recognised and DriveSpace will be used to read it or write to it. This process is not infallible, and if you find that a floppy appears to contain only one file called DRVSPACE.000 you can use the *Mount* option to allow it to be read.

Creating a compressed floppy is a slow process, and one way of speeding things up is to create one such floppy with the *AutoMount* option switched off, then copy the DRVSPACE.000 file to a folder on the hard drive. You can then use Explorer to copy this file to any other formatted blank floppy, making this floppy into a compressed one (because you have copied the compressed volume file). When you restore the *AutoMount* option of DriveSpace, these floppies will be recognised as compressed floppies, capable of holding up to 3 Mbyte of data each.

Note: Any compression system tends to slow down the computer because of the extra burden of work imposed on the processor. Now that hard drive prices are so low and manufacturers are fitting hard drives of at least 850 Mbyte as standard, the need for compression is much less, and if you need the fastest possible performance you should avoid it. This applies particularly to the Windows swap file, mentioned above.

- The advantage of using DriveSpace compression is that it allows you the continued use of older equipment with small hard drive(s). It also permits a floppy disc to hold the equivalent of files up to as much as 3 Mbyte in normal terms. You can, however, store even more on a floppy by using the **Backup** program.

- Never assume that because your compressed drive shows 100 Mbyte available that you can store 100 Mbyte of files in it. The available figure is an estimate that assumes a fixed compression ratio, often 2.0:1, and you cannot guarantee that your files can be compressed to this extent.

- You can use DriveSpace-3 (part of the Microsoft Plus! set) so that it eliminates the wasteful use of a complete hard drive cluster (which can be up to 32 Kbyte in size) to hold each small file. Using DriveSpace-3 with the compression ratio set as 1:1 will **not** compact the files themselves (so that no elaborate decoding is needed), but will eliminate the gaps in the clusters.

- -

Config.sys file

General: The CONFIG.SYS file is used during the process of starting up the computer, and is a file of commands that are executed before Windows 95 can be initiated. Another such file is called **AUTOEXEC.BAT**. You should not, in normal circumstance, need to edit or view the CONFIG.SYS file, because it is maintained automatically by Windows 95. If your computer was in use before Windows 95 was installed (using Windows 3.1 or DOS) then several portions of the file will have been modified by the installation program for Windows 95.

Editing: Start Notepad and use the Open command to look for all files (*.*). Look in the C:\ root folder and double-click CONFIG.SYS. The file can then be edited. See *BP319 MS-DOS 6 explained* for details of how to use this file.

Bypassing: If a command in the CONFIG.SYS file is causing problems with Windows 95, you can start the computer in such a way as to bypass the commands. Restart the computer, and when the *Starting Windows 95* message appears, press and release the F8 key. From the menu that appears, select *Step by Step Confirmation*. This allows you to accept or reject each step in the setup, starting with the CONFIG.SYS file. The final step should be the AUTOEXEC.BAT file (or Startup Command File, as it is referred to). If you do not use this file, you can avoid starting Windows 95 and the machine will be running DOS.

Notes: If you have never used DOS, and particularly if your computer was installed with Windows 95 when you bought it, you should never need to edit AUTOEXEC.BAT or CONFIG.SYS, and you should certainly not do so unless you understand the effects that changes in these files could cause.

Context-sensitive help

General: Much of the Help action in Windows 95 is context-sensitive, meaning that the help you get is related to the action you are trying to carry out at the time. The **?** icon at the top right-hand corner of a panel is used for this type of Help.

Copying objects

Seeking Help: Click on the ? icon. The ? sign will now appear next to the normal pointer, and you can click on the portion of the panel that you do not understand. A small explanatory panel will appear as a reminder of what to expect. An alternative is a Help menu item called *What's This*.

Notes: This type of Help is a very useful reminder, but it is necessarily brief, and is not useful if you are totally unfamiliar with the program actions that you are using.

. . . .

Copying objects

General: The normal *Cut/Copy* and *Paste* actions are provided in the *Edit* menu of any program running under Windows, but Windows also permits the use of the right-hand mouse button for a shortcut menu, and also the use of Drag and Drop editing in many programs. For a definition, see the entry for *object*. Note that the action described as *Move* is a copy action followed by deletion of the original object.

Shortcut menus: With some object (text, graphics, etc.) selected, click the right-hand mouse button over the selected area. You will see a short menu of the most-often-required actions. For text, this menu will typically be *Cut*, *Copy*, *Paste*, *Font*, *Paragraph*, *Bullets and Numbering*, and for graphics it will typically be *Cut*, *Copy*, *Paste*, *Format Drawing Object*, *Bring to Front*, *Send to Back*, *Send Behind Text*, *Group* and *Ungroup*. You can click *Copy* or *Cut* to copy selected text (using *Cut* will remove the text from its present position, making the *Cut* and *Paste* action a *Move*), and by clicking with the right-hand mouse button over another point in the document you can click the *Paste* portion of the menu and so paste in the copied material. The *Paste* action can be repeated.

Country (regional) settings

Drag and Drop: This action may need to be enabled for a specific program (for Word, in the Tools — Options — Edit menu) and is not available in other programs (such as Notepad of Windows 95). If Drag and Drop is available, select the text or graphics and keep the left-hand mouse button depressed until the cursor changes shape to its Drag and Drop form. Now drag the selected text or graphics to its new position, then release the mouse button. The action is normally a *Move* (*Cut and Paste*) type, but if you press the Ctrl key and hold it down during the dragging action, the action will be a *Copy and Paste*, so that the original text or graphic is not deleted.

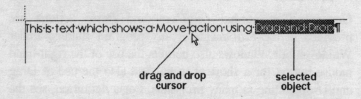

This·is·text·which·shows·a·Move·action·using Drag and Drop ¶

drag and drop   selected
cursor   object

Notes: The use of Drag and Drop is less attractive when the text or graphics object has to be moved over a large number of pages.

. . . .

Country (regional) settings

General: Windows 95 can be adapted to cater for differences between countries, something that is not always noted in books that originate in the USA. You can configure Windows by way of the *Regional Settings* of date, time, number format and currency sign and conventions.

Language settings: Use Start — Settings — Control Panel, or Control Panel from Explorer, and double-click on *Regional Settings*. The first tab deals with languages, offering the following main and auxiliary options:

Country (regional) settings

Afrikaans   Basque   Catalan

Danish   Dutch (Belgian)   Dutch (standard)

English (Australian)   English (British)   English (Canadian)

English (Caribbean)   English (Ireland)   English (Jamaica)

English (New Zealand)   English (South Africa)

English (USA)   Finnish   French (Belgian)

French (Canadian)   French (Luxembourg)

French (Standard)   French (Swiss)   German (Austria)

German (Liechtenstein)   German (Luxembourg)

German (Standard)   German (Swiss)   Icelandic

Indonesian   Italian (Standard)   Italian (Swiss)

Norwegian (Bokmal)   Norwegian (Nynersk)

Portuguese (Brazilian)   Portuguese (Standard)

Spanish (Argentina)   Spanish (Chile)

Spanish (Columbian)   Spanish (Costa Rica)

Spanish (Dominican Republic)   Spanish (Ecuador)

Spanish (Guatemala)   Spanish (Mexico)

Spanish (Modern)   Spanish (Panama)

Spanish (Paraguay)   Spanish (Peru)   Spanish (Traditional)

Spanish (Uruguay)   Spanish (Venezuela)   Swedish

Number settings: Several of the number settings, such as the use of a decimal point (rather than a comma) are fixed by your choice of language, but a few can be changed independently. The Panel displays examples of both positive and negative numbers as examples. The sections of this panel are *Decimal Marker, Number of Digits following Decimal*

Country (regional) settings

Marker, Digit Grouping Symbol, Number of Digits in Group, Negative Sign, Negative Number Format, Display Leading Zero, Measurement System and *List Separator*.

Using the English (British) Language setting, the default number of digits following the decimal point is 2, but you can select any number from 0 to 9. The digit grouping symbol is the comma, and the normal number of digits in a group is 3. The default negative number format uses the – sign ahead of the number, but you can opt for using brackets (for accountancy), to have the negative sign following the number, or to place a space between the negative sign and the number. There is no provision for using the longer – sign (the en-dash) that is usually required for mathematical typing in the UK, though this sign is available in Word and other programs that run using Windows 95.

Currency settings: Several of the currency settings are determined by the number settings which are in turn determined by language choice, and the only main item that can be varied is the negative number format, for which there are 15 options. The panel shows examples of positive and negative currency amounts and the options are *Currency Symbol, Position of Currency Symbol, Negative Number Format, Decimal Symbol, Number of Digits following Decimal Symbol, Digit Grouping Symbol* and *Number of Digits in Group*.

Time settings: The Panel shows an appearance sample, and for English (British) language setting the options for *Time Display* are HH:mm:ss (24-hour clock) or H:mm:ss (12-hour clock with AM and PM). The *Time Separator* is set as a colon (:), and the AM and PM letterings are fixed by the language choice.

Date settings: The Date panel has a *Calendar Type* setting which is fixed at *Gregorian Calendar* for most language

Date/Time

choices. The date options are grouped as *Short Date* or *Long Date*. The default *Short Date* style is dd/mm/yy, with three other options available, and the default separator is the slash (/). The *Long Date* has only the two options of dd MMMM yyy or d MMMM yyyy.

Notes: Other than checking the current date and time and the language setting when you install Windows, you need not use the *Regional Settings* again unless you have special requirements, such as using brackets to indicate negative numbers in accountancy, or typing documents that are intended for other countries and which must use different number and/or currency formats. If you use an accounts program it will configure its numbers independently of Windows 95.

Date/Time

General: The maintenance and display of Date and Time is handled by the *real-time clock* of the computer, called thus to distinguish it from the clock circuits that are used to synchronise the microprocessor actions. When re-setting is needed, the Date/Time panel can be used. Windows 95 will automatically alter the time by one hour to adjust between Winter Time and Summer Time.

Display: Click Start — Settings — Taskbar Options. If the option marked *Show Clock* is ticked, the time will be displayed at the right hand side of the Taskbar. Placing the pointer over the time display will show the date in long form (such as 19 June 1997).

Adjusting: The simplest method is to double-click the time in the Taskbar display if you have used the *Show Clock* option, or click the time with the right-hand mouse button and opt for *Date/Time* in the menu that appears. Alternatively, use

Defragmenting a hard drive

Explorer or My Computer to start the Control Panel and double-click *Date/Time*. You can change the year (beyond 2000 if required), month and day by clicking the arrowheads and the calendar display. To change time, click on the figure (hours, minutes or seconds) that you want to change and either click the arrowheads to adjust up or down or delete and type another number.

Time Zone: If you move to another Time Zone, click on this tab and select from the set of Time Zones that appears. The Time Zones are illustrated on a World map display, and also with examples of cities or countries in that time zone. The number of hours ahead of or behind GMT is also shown.

Summer Time: If you want Windows to change the hour automatically when Summer Time starts and ends, click the *Time Zone* tab and click to place a tick on the square labelled *Automatically adjust clock for daylight saving changes*.

Defragmenting a hard drive

General: When a file is deleted, its codes remain on the disc, but the space can from then on be used to store other files, replacing the bytes of the deleted file. If, however, the replacement files do not take up the same amount of space, there will be portions of the disc that are unused, and if a large number of files are saved, deleted and then replaced, the disc will start to suffer from fragmentation. On such a disc, saving a new file might make use of several portions of the disc that contained fragments of deleted files, and because the disc head has to move from portion to portion to read or write such a fragmented file, the time needed is longer. Defragmentation is a process which locates the fragments of files and stores them in adjacent parts of the disc, making access to such *contiguous files* quicker. To do this, files are read into memory and back to another part of the disc, and

42

the whole process can take several hours on a large disc. Windows 95 caters for defragmentation by using the System Tools Defragmenter.

Starting: Close down all programs. Click Start — Programs — Accessories — System Tools and then click on **Disk Defragmenter**. You will be asked which drive you want to defragment, the default is C:\. When you select a drive and click on the *OK* button, there will be a pause while the disc is checked, and a message will tell you how fragmented the disc is, and whether defragmentation is needed. If the fragmentation is 0% then you quite certainly do not need to use the defragmenter, but you may find that a drive with a fragmentation figure as low as 3% (with defragmentation not recommended in the message) can still show a gain in speed of use after defragmentation. Click the *Start* button to start the defragmentation of the selected disc.

Options: You can click the *Select Drive* button if you decide to defragment another drive instead (remember that if your hard drive is partitioned it will use more than one letter reference). Click the *Advanced* button to see options for the defragmentation process itself. There are three options for the process, labelled as *Full Defragmentation (Files and Free Space)*, which is the default. The other two are *Defragment Files Only* and *Consolidate Free Space Only*. You can check a box to make the defragmenter check the disc for errors before defragmenting (such errors are noted, so that the faulty parts of the drive will not be used again). Finally, you can opt to use your options this time, but revert to default next time, or to keep your options and make them the new default.

Note: You can follow the progress of defragmentation if you want to by clicking the button in the Defragmenter panel. Click also the button marked *Legends* for an explanation of the symbols that are used to represent clusters of data on the disc.

Deleting actions

- You **can** use the computer while defragmentation is proceeding, but there will be irritating pauses, and it is much better to start the process at a time when you do not need to use the computer. If you must use the computer, it is better to click the *Pause* button on the Defragmenter panel so that you can use the machine normally, with no hold-ups, and resume defragmentation when you are not using the machine.

- -

Deleting actions

General: You can delete text, files, folders, shortcuts and graphics. Unless you specify otherwise, deletion of objects is not permanent because they can be recovered from the Recycle Bin until the Bin is emptied. In other words, you do not clear any disc space by a delete action until the Recycle Bin is emptied. This provides for second thoughts if you need to replace something that you have deleted. Programs often have their own provision, such as the *Undo* icon of Word, for recovering deleted text or other items. You cannot delete the Recycle Bin but you can stop using it, see the entry for **Recycle Bin**.

Actions: All deletion starts with selection. Click on a file or folder name or on a graphic (so that the *handles* appear). If you work with the Desktop visible and the Recycle Bin displayed, you can drag the selected item to the Recycle Bin. If you work full-screen, which is more usual, press the Delete key. You will be asked to confirm that you want to send the selected item to the Recycle Bin.

- When you delete a folder you will automatically delete all the items that were contained in that folder. You will **not** be notified about individual items except for EXE files, to

44

remind you that you are deleting a program which you might possibly want to use.

Permanent deletion: If you are certain that you want to delete an item and you need the disc space, hold down the Shift key while you drag the item to the *Recycle Bin* or press the Delete key. You will be reminded that this is a deletion as distinct from a recycling. In some cases, you may see the *Recycle Bin* notice appear, and you need to click the *No* button and use Shift–Delete again. See the entry for **Recycle Bin** for permanent deletion of the files in this set.

....

Desktop

General: The Desktop display of Windows 95 appears in full when you minimise all programs, and can be partially seen when you run programs in small windows. If you use full-screen for your main programs, the desktop will not normally be visible, so that its appearance is not relevant. In addition, if the Desktop is not visible, you cannot use options such as dragging a file to the Recycle Bin or to a Printer icon, etc. The Desktop appearance can be altered in two main ways, *Background* and *Wallpaper*. The range of choices open to you may be determined by the options you used when setting up Windows 95.

Background: Click Start — Settings — Control Panel, or use Control Panel from Explorer. Double-click the *Display* option, and click on the *Background* tab. The illustration shows the effect on a blank desktop of the type of background you select. The list, obtained by using the scroll bar in the *Pattern* box, consists of:

None   50% Gray   Boxes   Bricks   Buttons   Cargo Net

Circuits   Cobblestones   Coliseum   Critters   Daisies

Desktop

Diamond   Dizzy   Field Effect   Key   Live Wire

Paisley   Pattern   Plaid   Quilt   Rounder   Scales

Scottie   Spinner   Stone   Thatches   Triangular

Tulip   Waffle   Waffle's Revenge   Weave

You can edit any pattern to make a new pattern which can be saved using another name. To edit a pattern click the *Edit Pattern* button and you will see a design of 8×8 squares. Click on a square to reverse its colour. When you have changed a pattern, you can click on the *Change* button to save this pattern under the existing file name. As an alternative, you can click the name and alter it, then use the *Add* button to add the new name for this altered pattern. If you want to delete a pattern, select it and click the *Remove* button. Click on the *Done* button to leave the editor panel.

Wallpaper: The Wallpaper options allows you the choice of *None* or several named varieties, including *Setup* – if no other names appear and you want to use Wallpaper you will need to use Windows 95 Setup to add the named wallpaper files. Wallpapers can be small images which are used by clicking the *Tile* option on the Panel, or large images which are used by clicking the *Center* option. If you use a centred Wallpaper option, you can use the Wallpaper along with any pattern, but patterns will not appear if you have opted to tile a Wallpaper.

If you see only *None* and *Setup* on your list of wallpapers, click the *Browse* button and look in C:\WINDOWS for the default full list, which is:

Clouds   Forest   Gold Weave   Metal Links   Red Blocks

Sandstone   Setup   Stitches

These are all BMP files which can be edited or created using Paint (see the **Paint** entry), and which will use the full range of colours that you have specified. Normally, if these files

Disc names

exist in C:\WINDOWS they will all appear in the list, but if you have BMP files in other folders, you can click the *Browse* button to look in these other folders and, if appropriate, add the files to your Wallpaper list.

Shortcuts on the Desktop: You can create shortcuts, placed on the Desktop, to any program or action or to a folder, floppy disc or printer. The easiest method is to minimise all programs other than Explorer, and use Explorer in a reduced window. Click the file, folder, program, printer or even another computer on a network, using the right-hand mouse button. When the menu appears, click *Make Shortcut*. For a file or folder, this will create a shortcut in the same folder that will appear selected, and you can then drag it to the Desktop. If you have selected a printer or disc then a notice will appear. The notice informs you that you cannot create the shortcut in the existing folder, and asks if you want it placed on the Desktop. Click the *Yes* button instead of dragging the shortcut to the Desktop.

For further information on Shortcuts, see the entry for **Shortcuts**.

Note: You can remove Shortcuts from the Desktop by selecting the shortcut and pressing the *Delete* key. This will send the Shortcut to the Recycle Bin. Alternatively, you can hold down the *Shift* key when you press *Delete* to make the deletion permanent.

Disc names

General: Each fixed drive or floppy disc can be named ('labelled') and the label name can be changed.

Method: Start My Computer by double-clicking on the icon. Click on the disc in the display that you want to rename, and then click File — Properties. Type the new name in the *Label*

Disc space

box, using up to 11 characters only. Click on the *OK* button to establish this new label name.

Notes: Names for drives or discs can be a useful reminder of your intentions. For example, if you use one hard drive for programs and another for data, using these names as labels will help to remind you when you see the drives listed in Explorer.

- -

Disc space

General: The *File Manager* program of Windows 3.1 always reported free disc space along with file size of a selected file, but Explorer is not so convenient to use in this respect, though there are several ways of reporting disc space.

Methods: Start My Computer, maximise the window, and click on the name of a disc drive. The display will show the number of Mbyte or Kbyte used, and the free space. The Explorer display will show disc free space when you click on a disc drive. If, however, you click on a filename to find the size of that file, you will no longer get the drive size when you click again on the drive unless you have clicked on another drive first.

You can get a more graphical display by clicking on any drive name with the right-hand mouse button and then clicking Properties in the menu. This will show a display of used and unused space for that drive. The same display is also available from the File — Properties menu of Explorer or of My Computer.

Notes: See also the details in the **My Computer** and **Explorer** entries.

Display

General: The Display item in Control Panel concerns the way that the monitor is used, and sets the Desktop appearance, as well as the resolution and colour range that can be used. Some Display items, such as Desktop are dealt with under separate entries, so that what follows concentrates on other aspects of the Display choices.

Panels: Click the Control Panel item in Explorer or use Start — Settings — Control Panel. Double-click on *Display*. The tabs that appear are labelled *Background, Screen Saver, Appearance*, and *Settings*. If you have installed Microsoft Plus! there will also be a tab labelled *Plus!*

Background: See the entry for **Desktop**.

Screen Saver: A Screen Saver is a pattern that replaces the normal screen display when the display remains unchanged for a set time. The theory is that this avoids 'burning in' a display on the screen, an effect you can see on the monitors that display arrivals and departures at airports. In practice, unless you leave the computer switched on with an unchanging screen display for really long periods, you are not likely to see burn-in in the lifetime of the computer – most computers are used for a couple of years before being replaced. Click on the *Screen Savers* tab to see what is available. The normal Windows set contains *Flying Windows, Marquee, Blank Screen*, and *None*. The *Blank Screen* saver is rather worse than none, because it gives the impression that the computer has been switched off, so that you should consider using *Flying Windows* or *Marquee*.

The *Flying Windows* saver displays moving Microsoft flags, along with buttons marked *Preview* and *Setting*, and a panel marked *Wait*. The *Wait* time (the time for which the screen display remains unchanged before triggering the Saver) can be changed to suit your requirements, and a useful setting is

Display

ten minutes. The *Settings* button can be clicked to bring up a speed and density selection. The speed setting is labelled *Warp Speed* (for Star Trek fans) and can be varied between limits of *Slow* and *Fast*. The *Density* figure refers to the number of flags on the screen, and can be varied between the limits of 5 and 75. Clicking on the *Preview* button will show for a short time how the effect looks on the full screen.

The *Marquee* display is of a scrolling message for which you can set the phrase to display along with font and speed. The Panel appearance is much the same as for *Flying Windows,* with the *Wait* time setting, but the *Settings* button leads to a very different set of choices. You can select the position for the message as *Centred* or *Random,* and you can select a *Background Colour*. The text itself can be typed into a box (which will scroll if needed), and you can set the *Speed* of scrolling on a *Slow* to *Fast* scale. A button labelled *Format Text* allows you to choose a font, colour and size of text, with options of *Strikeout* and *Underline*. Another option, *Script* applies only for a few font types – the default setting is *Western*. As before, you can use a *Preview* button on the main panel to see the full-screen effect.

- Other screensavers can be bought, and are often given away as part of a set of software bundled with a magazine. Check that any screensaver you obtain in this way is suitable for Windows 95.

Appearance: See the entries for **Fonts, Icons** and **ToolTips**.

Settings: This tab allows you to alter the resolution and colour range of your display, assuming that the monitor type is capable. The *Color Palette* setting will be 16 colours for standard VGA, with options of 256 colours, *High Colour* (16 bit) and *True Colour* (24-bit). The two latter settings demand a fast video card with 2 Mbyte of memory, and a monitor to match. The *Fonts* setting is of *Large Fonts* or *Small Fonts* –

use the *Small Fonts* settings for 640 × 480 resolution, and *Large Fonts* for higher resolution settings. You can also click the *Custom* button to set the font sizes for yourself from a ruler display that can be dragged to alter the number of pixels per inch. If you are using the higher-resolution settings, you can make the size of the displayed ruler match that of a real ruler held against the screen, ensuring that printed copy will be scaled to screen size. This may, however, cause some fonts to look much too small on a normal 14 inch monitor.

The resolution settings are altered by dragging a pointer over a scale labelled *Desktop Area*. The end of the scale marked *Less* will supply 640 × 480 resolution, VGA standard), and the end marked *More* will supply the maximum that your monitor can deliver, such as 800 × 600 or 1024 × 768. You can click a *Change Display* button to notify a change of monitor type and/or driver, but such changes are usually made when the **Add Hardware** action is being used.

Notes: The highest resolution settings are obtainable only if you are using a suitable monitor and driver, and unless you are changing only this aspect of your computer system you are stuck with the settings that were made when Windows 95 was installed.

Documents

General: A document, as far as Windows 95 is concerned, is a data file for a program, which might consist of text, of numbers, of graphics, sounds, or any mixture of these items. Windows 95 will keep a list of all suitable documents that have been opened, creating a shortcut so that you can quickly gain access to these documents again. Some older programs may create document types that do not appear in the list. You can open a document in its associated program by double-

Documents

clicking on the document name in the Explorer list, see the entry for **association**.

Document list: Adding a document is automatic and there is no provision for cancelling this action. To empty the document list, click Start — Settings — Taskbar — Start Menu and click the button (in the lower section) labelled *Clear*. You should clear the document list at frequent intervals.

Preview: You can preview any document provided that the *QuickView* program was installed with Windows 95. Click on the document name in Explorer, then on File — QuickView. If the *QuickView* item does not appear in the *File* menu, the item cannot be previewed, even if it has been associated with a program such as Notepad. You can, however, associate straightforward text files with *QuickView*, which is listed in the set of programs available for the **associate** action. See the **QuickView** entry for more details.

Send To: A document file can be sent to a floppy disc or to the printer by using Explorer. Start Explorer, select the document, and click File — Send To. This will display the choice of destinations, which can include networked drives. For more information, see the **Send To** entry.

Languages: The languages listed in the **country (regional) settings** entry are supported by Windows 95 automatically. If you want to work with documents that use languages originating in Central Europe, Greece, or Turkey, including Cyrillic or Baltic languages, you must install the multi-language support option. Close down all programs other than Explorer. Insert the Windows 95 CD-ROM or first floppy disc. Use *Control Panel* from the Start menu or from Explorer and double-click *Add/Remove Programs*. Select the *Windows Setup* tab, and click on *Multi-language Support*. Click the *Details* button to see the three support groups. The first deals with *Czech Republic, Hungarian, Polish and Slovenian*, the second with *Bulgarian, Belarusian and Russian*, and the third with *Greek*-based languages. Click on the OK button in each panel until the installation starts – if you install from floppies you will be prompted to insert the correctly numbered discs. You will be prompted to restart the computer so that the installation can be completed.

Icon: The icon for a document is determined by the type of document. In particular, if a document is associated with a program type, the icon for that type will be used. You may be able to change this icon as follows. From Explorer or My Computer, click View — Options and then click the *File Types* tab. Find the icon corresponding to the program that opens your document, and click the *Edit* button. The panel that appears contains the *Change Icon* option and you will usually find one or more optional icons available. Click on the icon you want to use (you can click on the *Default* button to restore the original icon). If you want to look through a larger list of icons, click the *Browse* button, and look for the file called MORICONS.DLL in the Windows folder. You can select an icon from the (large) set that appears.

Notes: Though a shortcut to a document needs only 1 Kbyte of disc space, remember that your hard drive is organised in clusters so that storing a 1 Kbyte file may require a 16 Kbyte or larger space. Maintaining a large documents list can therefore tie up a large amount of space on your hard drive.

Explorer

General: Explorer is the Windows 95 file and folder management program, corresponding to the File Manager of Windows 3.1. Using Explorer you can view contents of disc drives and folders, copy and move files, check properties of all items (from drives to files) and operate the Control Panel

Explorer

and the Recycle Bin. You can also change the My Computer display so that it uses the same two-panel system as Explorer, so making Explorer redundant. See the **My Computer** entry for details.

Starting: Click the Start button, followed by Programs — Windows Explorer. If Explorer is running when you quit Windows, it will be restarted the next time you switch on your computer – there is no need to keep a shortcut to Explorer in the Startup folder.

Display: The Explorer display consists of a tree on the left hand side and a folder/files list on the right hand side. The boundary can be dragged to left or right as you prefer. The tree diagram starts with Desktop and My Computer and displays the drives (hard, floppy, and CD-ROM), the Control Panel, Printer and Recycle Bin.

Tree display: The tree display at the left hand side shows each section of the Explorer tree as a list of drives and main folders, and a box with a + sign indicates that further information is available by clicking the box. For example, clicking the box for a hard drive will result in expanding the tree diagram to show the folders of the hard drive, with a corresponding display of folders and files in the right-hand side. Click again on the box to collapse the tree again. In this way you can see as much detail as you want – this is particularly useful if you use more than one hard drive, or a drive which has been partitioned into two or more parts. You can also select a drive and press the asterisk key (*) on the numeric keypad – this will have the effect of opening out all folders, equivalent to clicking on each + sign in the folders for that drive. You can also double-click a folder to open out a display of its sub-folders.

Files and Folders display: The display of folders and files on the right-hand side of the Explorer window can be tailored to your requirements by using the View menu. You can opt for a set of icons only by clicking on *Large Icons* or *Small Icons*. The other options produce lists, and the *List* option shows much the same set of icons and names as the *Small Icons* set, but with the arrangement sorted vertically into columns rather than horizontally into rows. The *Details* option is particularly useful, because it shows *Size*, *Type* and *Modification Date* for all files. The Line Up Icons action is available only if the Large Icons or Small Icons display is in use.

Icons can be arranged in order, and an *Autoarrange* option is available if you have selected *Large Icons* or *Small Icons*. All arrangements show folders sorted ahead of files. The other arrangements, which are also available when you select a list, are to sort in order of *Name*, *Type*, *Size* and *Date*. The *Name* arrangement sorts into alphabetical order of main filename, and the *Type* order sorts in order of extension letters. The *Size* and *Date* options are particularly useful if you want to find very large or very small files, or to find your oldest or newest files. A sort arrangement will remain in place until you cancel it.

View Options: The View — Options menu allows you to select three useful choices. Click on the box marked *Display Full MS-DOS Path in Title Bar* if you want to see the full path for your files – this is useful if you are going to start an MS-DOS program. The second box is labelled *Hide MS-DOS File Extension for File Types that are Registered*. This shows the main file names only, and makes for a less-cluttered display, providing that you remember the icon shapes for different file types. The third box is labelled *Include Description Bar for Right and Left Panes*, and ticking this box will ensure that your Explorer panels have headings such as *All Folders* and *Contents of 'C:'*.

Copy and Move: The *Copy* and *Move* actions are most

easily carried out by dragging. The default action is that dragging a file between folders on the same hard (or floppy) drive is **always** a move action, but dragging between two different drives (such as floppy disc and hard drive folder) is **always** a copy action. Select the file or folder to be copied or moved and drag it to the new position.

- If you want to enforce a copy action in a drag between folders on the same drive, hold down the Ctrl key when you start a drag action. If you want to enforce a move action between the hard drive and a floppy, hold down the Shift key when you start a drag action.

- If the destination for your drag action is not in view, drag to the top or the bottom of the Directories display panel so that this part of the display scrolls. It is easier to locate your target folder if you ensure that it is visible before you start dragging.

Rename: To rename a file or folder, click on the name so that it is selected. Wait, and then click again. On the second click, a frame will appear around the name, and you can delete the name and type another. Alternatively, you can use the cursor arrow keys to delete part of a name and then retype a portion. Press the RETURN key, or click somewhere else, to establish the new filename.

New file/folder: With a drive or folder selected, click on File — New and when the options appear, on *File* or *Folder* (or on any of the specified types that are listed). The new file or folder will appear in a drive or folder listing, with a default name ready to edit so that you can type in whatever name you want to use (then press the RETURN key or click elsewhere).

Run program: Double-click on a program name to start it running. If the program is an MS-DOS type, it will run in an MS-DOS window, see later. If you double-click on a document file name which is associated with a program, the program will start with the document opened. You can also use the File — Open menu item.

Refresh display: When files have been added to a folder by other methods (that is, not using Explorer) the Explorer display can be updated either by pressing the F5 key or by using the View — Refresh menu action.

Properties: The *Properties* of Folders or Files can be changed using the Explorer display. Select a file or folder, and click File — Properties. For a Folder you will see a single panel containing entries for *Type*, *Location*, *Size* and *Contains*. The *MS-DOS File Name* will appear, with, if appropriate, a *Created* date. The attributes of *Read-only*, *Hidden*, *Archive* and *System* will appear as boxes that are ticked if the attribute is set. The *System* box is greyed out to prevent alteration.

The display for files can be more complex. In general, document files and some types of program files use only the same *General* panel as is used for Folders, but many document files, particularly from Word, also contain tabs marked *Summary* and *Statistics* that provide additional information on the contents of the file.

Some program files, and in particular, MS-DOS program files, use up to six tabs. Programs that run under Windows have a *Version Tab* on their *Properties* set. This shows information on the use of the file, and has an information list with headings of *Company Name*, *Internal Name*, *Language*, *Original Filename*, *Product Name* and *Product Version*. Click on a name to see the related information. The *Product Name* information can sometimes be a useful way of finding if a file is needed – you may find, for example, that it is used as part of a set that you do not need.

• For the MS-DOS program set, which can be ignored if

Explorer

you do not use MS-DOS programs, see the **MS-DOS** entry.

Shortcuts: You can create a shortcut to a file by dragging it to a new location with the Ctrl and Shift keys both held down. Alternatively, you can drag with the right-hand mouse button held down and select *Shortcut Here* from the menu that appears.

Menu items: The Explorer menus provide some alternatives to actions that can be carried out faster using the mouse, and some actions that cannot be carried out using the mouse. The File menu contains *Open, QuickView, Send To, New, Create Shortcut, Delete, Rename, Properties* and *Close*. The *QuickView, Send To,* and *New* items are separate entries in their own right in this book, and there are faster options for the other actions. If you have selected a document file which has no association, the *Open* item will become *Open With* so that you can select a program to use in opening the file. The *File* menu also contains *New*, which will create a new folder or a new shortcut If you use Microsoft Office, the *New* list will also show a selection of Office document types.

In the *Edit* menu, the *Undo* action can be used to reverse some step, such as deletion or renaming, that you have had second thoughts about. The type of action (*Undo Delete, Undo Rename*) is specified. The menu options of *Cut, Copy* and *Paste* are also contained here with reminders of their key options of Ctrl-X, Ctrl-C and Ctrl-V respectively. The *Paste Shortcut* item is used when you have copied or cut a shortcut from another location and you want to place the shortcut into the current folder. Two particularly useful commands are *Select All*, which will select all the files in the current folder, and *Invert Selection* which will deselect all the selected files in a folder and select the files which were not previously selected.

The Tools menu contains *Find* and *GoTo*, both of which have entries of their own in this book.

Notes: Explorer is very versatile, and you should keep it available each time you start Windows by ensuring that it is running when you quit Windows.

• Former Windows 3.1 users complain that the double-window system of File Manager was more useful. File Manager can be used with Windows 95, but it ignores long filenames, and has not the range of actions of Explorer. Remember that you can drag selected files from any Explorer files display to any folder because the files display does not change unless you double-click on a folder name on the left-hand panel. If is therefore possible to select files in one folder and to scroll the left-hand panel to show any other drive or folder to which the files can be dragged.

- -

Extract

General: The Extract utility is not a well-documented part of Windows 95, and it requires using MS-DOS mode. It is, however, the only reasonable way of restoring a Windows file that you have deleted accidentally and which is not available as one of the identifiable files on the CD-ROM or the floppy set. You will need to place the Windows 95 CD-ROM or floppy disc set into the appropriate drive.

Using: Switch to MS-DOS mode and change drive to your CD-ROM drive or floppy drive using, for example D: or A: as the command followed by pressing the RETURN key. The format of the EXTRACT command will be summarised if you type EXTRACT and press the RETURN key. For most purposes, you can use the command in the form:

EXTRACT /A /L *destination* D:\WIN95\WIN95_02. CAB *filename*

File types

where *destination* means the folder where you want the file to be added, D is the CD-ROM drive in this example, and *filename* is the name of the file that you have lost. There must be a space between each section of the command. Press the RETURN key to carry out the action. The /A addition to the command will cause all CAB files to be searched starting with the one that you specify (in this case, WIN95_02.CAB, which is the first CAB file on the CD-ROM). For floppy discs you will have to specify the A: drive and the number of the first CAB file that appears.

Example: The command (typed in one line though illustrated on two lines here because of its length):

EXTRACT /A /L C:\WINDOWS\SYSTEM
F:\WIN95\WIN95_02.CAB MFC30.DLL

will extract the file called MFC30.DLL (used to open font files) from the CAB files on a Windows 95 CD-ROM, using a CD-ROM drive lettered F, searching all CAB files, and placing the MFC30.DLL file in the folder C:\WINDOWS\SYSTEM

Notes: This action is one that you should seldom need, but it is a much more satisfactory solution to the problem of a missing file than a complete re-installation of Windows.

File types

General: Each program that you have installed will create or use data files, and the extension letters for these files describe the type of file (such as DOC for WORD text, or TXT for ASCII files). When you install a new program, its file types will be added to the list that Windows keeps, but if you simply import some files from a floppy this adding to the types list does not take place. You can add the files, using methods that are used for association.

Adding a new file type: Starting in Explorer or My Computer, click View — Options — File Types, you will see a list of registered file types. Click on any file type to see the extension letters of the data file and the program that can be used to open the file. Click on the *New Type* button. Click in the *Description of Type* box and type a brief description – this will appear in Explorer if you have specified to see details of files. Click in the *Associated Extension* box and type the extension letters that your new file type uses.

You can then specify what actions you require, usually *Open* and *Print*. Click the *New* button to see the *New Action* panel. Type the action (such as *Open*) and, in the *Application* space, specify the program that will carry out this action. For example, to open a BMP file you could specify Paint. Use the *Browse* button to find the program you want to use and click the *Open* button to establish this as the required program. There is a box marked *Use DDE* which can be ticked if the program manual advises you to do so.

When you return to the main panel your action will appear entered, and you can click the *Use QuickView* box if you want to be able to use *QuickView* on this type of file.

Remove file type: Click on the file type in the View — Options — File Types display. You will be reminded that removing the file from the list will make it inaccessible by double-clicking. The list usually contains a large number of files that you would not normally start in that way.

Change Icon: You can click the *Change Icon* button in the *View Types* list to see the range of icons that are available. For a new file, you can choose from a set contained in a file called SHELL32.DLL which is contained in the folder C:\WINDOWS\SYSTEM. You can also use the *Browse*

Filenames

button to use another icon file, such as the icons file C:\WINDOWS\MORICONS.DLL. Click on an icon to use it as the icon for the selected file type.

Notes: While using the *Edit* option, you can click the box marked *Always Show Extension* to ensure that this file type is always shown with its extension letters even if you have opted not to show the extension letters of files.

Filenames

General: Windows 95 allows the use of long filenames, not confined to the older MS-DOS convention of up to 8 characters of main name and up to 3 characters in the extension.

Naming/Renaming file: A file can be named when it is saved, usually using the *Save As* option of the program which created the file. For a Windows 95 program, you can use a filename of up to 255 characters (including folder names in the path), and the filename can include spaces and full-stops, unlike the older MS-DOS standard. The characters \ / : * ? " < > | are forbidden and must not be used. A long filename can also be used when a file is renamed (see entry for Explorer).

Alias name: When a Windows 95 file is named, using a long name, an alias name that corresponds to MS-DOS standards is also created. For example, a file called Ian Sinclair.doc has an MS-DOS alias of IANSIN~1.DOC. The alias is created by using the first six valid characters of the long filename, adding the ~ symbol, and a digit that distinguishes files which have the same first six characters. If the long filename contains, within its first six characters, one that cannot be used in an MS-DOS filename, the alias will be shortened to avoid using that character. To see an alias name, click the file in an Explorer display and use File — Properties. The

General panel will show the alias under the title of *MS-DOS Name*.

Note: In some circumstances, when you add a new hard drive of more than 512 Mbyte to an older computer (usually a 486 type manufactured in or around 1994) you may find that the new drive will not store files that use a long filename. The remedy is to use a different driver, and most hard drives will come with software that includes a suitable driver for these machines.

Find

General: The Find action is available from the *Start* button menu or from the *File* menu of My Computer when a drive has been selected. Any file or folder that exists on a hard drive, or on a CD-ROM or floppy that has been inserted, can be found, and search conditions can be typed and saved if a similar search is likely to be wanted again. Files that have been deleted (to the Recycle Bin) can be found and retrieved provided that the Bin has not been emptied.

Starting Find: From Explorer, click Tools — Find — Files or Folders. From My Computer, click File — Find. From the Start button, click Find — Files or Folders.

Specifying a search: When Find starts, you will see the three-part specification panel, but for many types of searches you need only the Name and Location Panel. More elaborate searches are needed if you are working on a network. Fill in the filename, or part of the filename that you are looking for in the *Named* box. If you know only part of a name, represent the rest with one or more asterisks. For example, you can type IAN*.DOC if you know only the first three letters and the extension, or MOR*.* if you know the first three letters only. Click the arrowhead to see some items that have been used in previous searches.

Find

The *Look In* section is used to specify the search area. If you have absolutely no idea where the file/folder might be located, use *My Computer* in *Look In*. This will ensure that all drives are searched, and is particularly useful if you have more than one hard drive, or a partitioned drive, with data in all portions. If, however, you know that the type of file you are looking for is in one particular drive you can save time by specifying this, such as D:\. You may even be able to select a folder that you feel certain contains the file you want to find. Always ensure that the box marked *Include Subfolders* is ticked.

- You can click the arrowhead in the *Look In* portion to see other locations, and you can use the *Browse* button to find a specific folder to search.

When you have specified your file as closely as you can, click the *Find Now* button to carry out the search. The results, showing file paths, will appear in a window that opens up beneath the *Find* panel. The *View* menu options can be used (in the same way as in Explorer) to determine how the files are displayed.

Options: A search is more difficult if no part of the filename can be recalled. The *Date Modified* section of *Find* allows you to specify by date. The default option is *All Files*, but you can alter this by clicking on *Find All Files Created or Modified* allowing you to specify a range of dates in the *Between* option, or a prior time using *During the Previous Months* or *During the Previous Days*.

The *Advanced* panel allows you to specify registered file types (see the file type entry). The default is *All Files and Folders*, but you can click the arrowhead to select any file type that is registered in your copy of Windows. For files that contain, or consist of, text, you can type a fragment of text in the *Containing Text* box. If you know (roughly) the size of the file, you can opt for the *Size Is* box, clicking to select *At Least* or *At Most*, and using the twin arrowheads to fill in a size in Kbyte.

Menus: The File menu of Find contains, after a search has been carried out, *Open*, *Open with WordPad*, *Print*, *New*, *QuickView*, *Send To*, *Create Shortcut*, *Delete*, *Rename*, *Properties*, *Open Containing File*, *Save Search* and *Close*. If no search has been carried out, only the last seven of the items are listed, and only a few of these are available.

The *Open* action will open a file, and the more specialised *Open with WordPad* can be used to open a text document using *WordPad* (even if the document is associated with another program). *Print* will print the document, using the print action of the program that created the file, and *New* loads a selected document file into a program and allows you to edit it.

The *QuickView* action allows you to see a portion of a data file before you decide that it is the one you want to use – this is particularly useful if your search has produced a large number of files. You can use *Send To* to print or save the file on another disc or drive (depending how you have set up the *Send To* action), and *Create Shortcut* can be used to place a shortcut to the file in any folder that you specify. The *Delete*, *Rename* and *Properties* actions correspond to the Explorer actions.

The *Open Containing Folder* action is useful if you think it would be useful to see the folder that contains the file you have selected from the search. *Save Search* can be clicked to save the criteria (or both criteria and results) for a search. The saved search is put as a shortcut on the Desktop rather than as a file that can be read by *Find*. If you tick the *Save Results* in the *Options* menu of *Find* the results of a search

Floppy discs

will be saved as well as the criteria.

The *Edit* menu consists of *Undo*, *Cut*, *Copy*, *Select All* and *Invert Selection*, all corresponding to the commands in Explorer. The *View* menu is the same as that of Explorer. The *Options* menu contains *Case Sensitive* which is useful if a file name contains both lowercase and uppercase letters, and the *Save Results* option.

Notes: When a search has been carried out, you can clear it by clicking the *New Search* button. This will clear the results of the previous search, and you can then click *Find Now* to start a new search with new criteria.

Floppy discs

General: The floppy disc is still the primary backup method for data files, and the main distribution method for software, despite its limited capacity, though floppy discs of 100 Mbyte capacity are in development. The capacity of the ordinary 3½" disc, nominally 1.4 Mbyte, can be considerably increased by using DriveSpace, see the **Compressed drive** entry.

Use: The floppy drive appears as an icon in the My Computer and Explorer displays. You can copy a file from any hard drive folder to the floppy by dragging it to the floppy disc icon. With the floppy drive selected, click the File — Properties item to check the state of the disc (used and unused space) and to activate tools for checking disc surface.

Format: To format a new disc (excluding DriveSpaced discs), open My Computer, select the floppy drive, and use File — Format. This opens a panel that starts with the capacity figure that is, by default, 1.4 Mbyte, and you would normally format all discs to this figure (see note below). The Format options are *Quick*, which is suitable for reformatting a disc that has been previously formatted and used, *Full*, for a new disc or one that has been formatted to a different size, and *Copy System Files* only, used for a formatted disc to be used as an MS-DOS system disc (see also **Startup Disc** entry).

• Note that if you place a nominal 720 Kbyte floppy (with only one hole) into your drive and use the Full Format command from My Computer, you can format such a disc as a 1.4 Mbyte disc. This saves the effort of drilling the additional hole, but the disc may not be recognised by older computers running DOS or earlier versions of Windows.

The other options are to type in a label name (no more than 11 characters), to specify that *No Label* name will be used, to *Display Summary when Finished* and to *Copy System Files Only*.

Copy disc: A floppy disc can be copied to another floppy in one action even if the computer contains only one floppy drive, and this action is important if you want to make backups of your original distribution discs for important programs. To copy a disc, put the disc that contains the files in the drive, and use My Computer. Select the drive, and click on File — Copy Disc. You will see a panel that contains two sections, both labelled with the letter for the floppy drive (usually A:). When the progress indicator reached half-way you will be prompted to place a blank formatted disc into the drive to complete the copying action.

• You can continue using the computer while copying is going on, but there is a risk that when the *Change disc* notice appears you may press a key that starts the copy to the disc that is already in the drive.

Installing from: To install a new Windows 95 program from the floppy drive, you should unless advised otherwise use the

Fonts

Control Panel and double-click *Add/Remove Programs*. Place the first (or only) disc into the drive. Click the *Install* key, and unless the A: drive is automatically used, specify this drive. The action will search for a file called INSTALL or SETUP and display it, so that you can start the installation. If more than one disc is used in a set, you will be prompted to replace discs as the installation proceeds.

Installing a modern Windows 95 program in this way will allow the program to be removed (uninstalled) later, provided that no files are deleted manually. Many older programs carry on their disc labels the instructions to insert the disc in the drive, click Start — Run and type a name such as A:\INSTALL or A:\SETUP. The *Add/Remove Programs* method can be used for these discs, but it will not be possible to remove the program later except by manual methods (locating the files and deleting them).

Notes: See the entry for **compressed drive** for details of using Drivespace to extend the capacity of a floppy.

* You can use the File — Create Shortcut menu item of My Computer, with the floppy drive selected, to place a shortcut to the floppy drive on the Desktop.

Fonts

General: A font is a design for printed characters. Font designs can be serif or sans-serif. A serif font uses a more elaborate design, with small 'hooks' at the ends of letters. The sans-serif fonts use plain designs in which it can be difficult to distinguish the letter 'ell' from the numeric 'one'. Serif fonts are used for long text items, because a serif font is more readable. Sans-serif fonts are used to break up the monotony of long text, particularly for captions and quotes, and also for short documents. Windows 95 keeps fonts in a folder of their own, and has several font-management facilities so that you can use your fonts in all of your Windows programs. Large collections of fonts, typically 1500 or more, are available on CD-ROM.

Using fonts: By default, the text that you see in Windows (such as menu names and lists) uses a sans-serif font. You can change this by using the Control Panel, either from Explorer or from Start — Settings — Control Panel. Double-click *Display*, and use the *Appearance* tab. The Item panel contains a list of the essential parts of a window, several of which (such as title bar, icon, menu, etc.) use fonts. For each item that uses a font, you can click the arrowhead on the *Font* space to see the list of fonts available to you. You can then change the font and the size (see **Notes**, below).

You may not like the effect of your changes unless you remember that small sizes of serif fonts do not look clear on a 640 × 480 screen, and that a change of colour of font or background can often make a font look clearer. Printed work always looks better than its appearance on the screen might suggest.

TrueType fonts: Your programs that make use of fonts will be able to select from the set of fonts that you install with Windows 95 and any fonts that you subsequently add. You should use fonts from the TrueType set for any document that will be printed, because the printout of such fonts matches their screen appearance – this cannot be guaranteed for the ordinary screen fonts that are not marked with the T_T logo.

Adding/Removing: Fonts can be added or removed using the Control Panel. Double-click on the *Fonts* icon and wait until the *Fonts* menu appears. To add a font, you will need a floppy or CD-ROM that contains fonts. Click on File — Install New Font. You will see the *Fonts* installation panel appear, with a list of fonts (blank), and boxes for *Folder* and

Fonts

Drive. You will need to change the drive and folder entries to match the source of your new fonts (floppy or CD-ROM), and when you do this the names of the new fonts will appear in the fonts list. You can select one or more fonts. If you want to install all of the fonts from a set, click on the *Select All* button. Make sure that the box marked *Copy fonts to Fonts folder* is ticked, and then click on the *OK* button.

To delete a font, use the *Font Manager* as above and select the name of the font you want to delete. Click the *Delete* key or use File — Delete. You will not be able to select a font if you have opted to *Hide Font Variations* (see Font management, following).

Font Management: The *Font Manager* of Control Panel allows you to use some actions that are not available from other menus. The File menu contains *Open*, *Print*, *Install New Font*, *Create Shortcut*, *Delete*, *Rename* and *Properties*. Of these, *Open* and *Print* are used to show the appearance of fonts on a sample page, and cannot be used unless the file MFC30.DLL is present in the WINDOWS\SYSTEM folder. The *Install* option has been dealt with, above, and the other actions on selected font files correspond to the Explorer actions of the same name.

The *Edit* menu also corresponds to that of Explorer, but there are some items in the View menu that are unique to Font Manager. *List Fonts by Similarity* allows you to pick one font in the heading of a list, and show the other fonts graded *as Very Similar*, *Fairly Similar*, *Not Similar* or *No PANOSE Information Available*. This type of listing is useful if you are trying to match fonts. The *Hide Variations* option can be selected so that each font is shown as a single entry, ignoring style variations such as Normal, Bold, Italic, and so on. This makes the fonts list look rather less daunting.

The *Options* set of View contains a panel with four tabs.

Click the *Folder* tab to see two options for viewing multiple folders. You can use a separate window for each folder (the default) or use a window whose contents change for each folder – this latter option makes it much easier to close down the folder window. The *View* tab and *File Types* tab correspond to the same displays in Explorer, and the *TrueType* tab allows you to show only the TrueType fonts in the Font Manager display

Notes: Font size is measured in terms of point, with one point equal to $1/72$". The size is the **height** of any capital letter (because lower-case letters are not all of the same height), and because of the differing designs of fonts, you can find that a sentence typed using several different fonts of the same point size will take up surprisingly different amounts of space, because of the different width of letters in different fonts but of the same point size.

GoTo

General: The GoTo action is intended to provide a quick method of opening a folder, but you need to know the path in terms of drive letter and intermediate folders.

Action: From Explorer (or an Explorer window in My Computer) click on Tools — GoTo. Fill in the path to the folder you want to open and click the *OK* button. The folder contents will be displayed on the right-hand panel of the Explorer display.

Note: If you do not know how to find the folder, use the Tools — Find action instead of *GoTo*, clearing the tick from the *Search Subfolders* box.

Hardware

Hardware

General: When Windows 95 is installed, it keeps a record of all the hardware (drives, monitor, modem, printer, etc.) that exists at that time. If you subsequently change your hardware you need to do so in a way that ensures that these records (see the entry for **registry**) are correctly maintained. This must be done after the mechanical work of bolting in and connecting a new piece of hardware has been satisfactorily completed. You can, however, remove hardware from the records without physically removing the equipment.

Adding hardware: Use Control Panel from Explorer or from Start — Settings — Control Panel. Double-click on *Add New Hardware*. This starts the title panel of a Wizard, and you need to click the *Next* button. The next panel asks if you want to have Windows automatically detect your new hardware. This is the advised option, because if Windows detects the hardware it will almost certainly ensure that the correct software driver is installed. If you opt for manual detection then you will probably need a disc containing drivers from the supplier of the new hardware.

The type of hardware that can be detected is listed as:

CD-ROM controller	Display Adapter	Floppy disc controller
Hard drive controller	Keyboard	Memory Technology Driver
Modem	Mouse	Multi-function adapter
Network adapter	Other device	PCMCIA socket
Port (LPT or COM)	SCSI controller	Sound, Video, Games controller

System Devices

Before you start to use the auto-detect action, shut down all programs other than Explorer. When you start the auto-detect action, the progress is indicated by a bar-graph display, and the action may take several minutes. Do not worry if there is no change in the indicator for a minute or so, as long as you can hear your hard drive working. When the action is completed you will see a report on the new hardware that Windows has detected and on the driver that has been used.

If Windows does not detect a new hardware item, or if you opt for manual detection, you will see a list of manufacturers and equipment from which you can select. Click the *Have Disc* button to install a driver that has been supplied by a manufacturer, and be guided by the Wizard.

Hardware conflicts: If a new item of hardware refuses to operate correctly this may be due to conflicts, usually when older hardware is in use. Windows 95 can help to resolve such conflicts by using a Wizard called the *Hardware Conflict Troubleshooter*. Click this item in the *Help* index and then click on the box labelled *Start the Hardware Conflict Troubleshooter*. Follow the instructions that appear in each step until the problem is resolved.

Hardware profiles: These are files that are used to allow Windows to adapt to different configurations and which apply mainly to portable machines whose hardware connections depend on whether the machine is docked or free. This is a specialised topic which needs experience, and will not be covered in this book.

Note: You do not need to use *Add Hardware* if you add another hard drive to your system, only if you change the hard drive controller. See also the entry for **Plug and Play**.

Help

General: On-screen help is available on many topics, but the information can often be patchy, and sometimes you find that

Help

you are switching between panels without getting any useful advice. Some of the most useful help is the **context-sensitive** type (see entry), and where this is not indicated by a question-mark icon, it may be found as a *What's This* item in the Help menu.

Starting help: Click the *Help* menu on the header bar, or press the F1 key. You will see the *Help* menu for Windows 95 if no other program is active. If you fetch the wrong *Help* set (from Word, for example), minimise all programs so that you see the Desktop of Windows 95. The other route to Windows 95 Help (which provides Windows 95 Help even if other programs are running) is Start — Help.

Help Topics: When the main Help window appears, it is divided into *Contents*, *Index* and *Find*. The *Contents* section is aimed at the newcomer to Windows, and the initial window shows the topics of *Tour, Introducing Windows, How To..., Tips and Tricks* and *Troubleshooting*. Double-click on an item represented by the book icon to expand it, and double-click on other (book icon) items that appear in an expanded list to find the advice.

The more experienced user will normally use the *Index* section. In the header of this window, you can delete any default text with the *Delete* key and start to type the words you are looking for. As you type, corresponding *Help* items will be selected, and you can click on the *Open* button to show the *Help* notes associated with that item. Cross-referencing is used, so that the same topic can be reached by typing different words. For example, you can find the same Help item by typing *fixing errors in discs* or by typing *discs repairing*.

The *Find* tab starts a form of database which scans the *Help* files for words that you type. This is not exactly foolproof – you will get advice on fixing disc errors, for example if you type *fix*, but not when you have completed typing *fixing*. The *Options* button can be used to determine how you want to make use of the letters that you have typed. The first section is headed *Search for Topics Containing* and the default option is *All the words you typed in any order*. The other options are *At least one of the words you typed* and *The words you typed in exact order*. There is a check box labelled *Display matching phrases* which will show in the display the words that follow the phrase that you typed. This makes the search slower but helps to locate what you want.

The *Show Words that* section contains as its default *begin with the characters you typed*, but you can click the arrowhead to use the options of *contain the characters you typed*, *end with the character you typed* and *match the characters you typed*. In the *Begin Search* section you can opt for *After you Click the Find Now Button* or *Immediately After a Keystroke*. The checkbox in this section is labelled *Wait for a Pause Before Searching* and applies only if you opt for searching immediately after a keystroke.

The buttons of the *Options* panel are *OK*, *Cancel* and *Files*. Click the *Files* button to narrow the search down to one or more of the *Specialised Help files* (which are all selected by default, with a *Select All* button to use if you have selected a single file and want to search all).

Help on Top: *On Top* means that a *Help* window will always appear over any other window, so that the *Help* text is never covered unless you drag the *Help* window out of sight. With a *Help* topic window displayed, click on *Options*. Click the *Help on Top* item, and then click *On Top* so that this option is ticked. If you click *Default*, some *Help* windows will be on top and others not. You can click *Not on Top* if you want *Help* windows to be covered by other windows that are opened later.

Help

Help Options: The *Options* button of a *Help* window contains the *Help on Top* item as noted above, and several other useful items. The *Annotate* option allows you to make notes about a *Help* item that can be displayed when that item is called up. When you use this option by clicking *Annotation*, you will see a panel appear into which you can type your note. The buttons beside the panel are labelled *Save, Cancel, Delete, Copy* and *Paste*. Use the *Save* button when you have completed your note, or use *Cancel* if you have second thoughts. *Delete* is used when you want to erase an existing note. *Copy* is used to copy selected text in the *Annotation*, and *Paste* can be used if you have copied other text to the Clipboard and want to paste it into the *Annotation* space. When an annotation existing in a *Help* panel, a paper-clip symbol appears next to the title of the *Help* panel. Click on this symbol to display the annotation.

The *Copy* option is used to copy selected *Help* text to the Clipboard. Once this has been done, you can paste the text into another program such as Notepad or Word. The *Print Topic* option will print the whole of a *Help* panel (the printer must be switched on and on line). A new page will be taken for each topic. The *Font* options allows you to specify *Small, Normal* or *Large* font size for the text in the *Help* panel. Finally, the *Use System Colors* option can be clicked so that the colours used in *Help* match the colour scheme you are using for other items. When you alter this *Colors* option, you will have to close the *Help* file and restart it to see the effect.

Note: The *Back* button in a *Help* panel can be used to return to the last *Help* panel you opened (not to the index). Return to the index by clicking on the *Help Topics* button.

HyperTerminal

General: HyperTerminal is a communications program that would take a complete book in its own right to explain thoroughly. What follows is simply a brief outline of its capabilities. You computer must be fitted with a modem, correctly installed, to make use of HyperTerminal. You may not need to use HyperTerminal – for example, if you want access to the Internet or to E-mail, there are specialised programs that are much more suitable. You can use HyperTerminal for making access to bulletin boards or to other computer services that are accessible on telephone numbers that you know.

Starting HyperTerminal: Click on Start — Programs — Accessories — HyperTerminal Connections. This does **not** launch HyperTerminal right away but displays a set of files of which one is **Hypertrm**, the terminal program. When you **double-click** on this file the terminal program will start. This is one of the few examples where double-clicking is needed for a program launched from the Start menu.

- You could make a shortcut direct to Hypertrm if you are likely to make use of the program frequently.

Note that if you want to switch between HyperTerminal and other programs you should click on the HyperTerminal window or use the Alt-Tab method, because clicking on the HyperTerminal icon in the Taskbar will bring you back to the folder which contains the Hypertrm program.

You are asked to type a name which will be used for the *session file* that keeps track of how you want to use HyperTerminal for one particular connection. You will need to create a file for each different contact, and in the example that follows we'll look at how to connect to a bulletin board in the UK. You will be asked for a filename, and the name of

77

the bulletin board is appropriate here.

You will then see the next form which requires the country code, area code and telephone number. The connection is shown as *Standard modem* (or whatever name of modem you use), with alternatives of *COM1* to *COM4* if you are connected directly through one of these ports. In this form, you can fill in the number for the bulletin board. You can opt not to use Country and area codes if you are using a local number.

You will need to omit the first zero in the area code. The zero is supplied as part of the country code, so if you use the zero in the area code you will always get voice messages about unrecognised numbers. If your modem has no loudspeaker you will not hear these announcements.

You will now see a *Connect* panel, showing the number that you want to dial. There will be an additional 0 shown spaced from the other digits, but this does not interfere with the dialling unless you have started the area code with a zero. Your location is shown as *Home*, so that HyperTerminal will know that you are making a call within the UK. The *Modify* button allows you to alter the phone number if you want to, and also provides for altering some terminal actions by way of a *Settings* panel. These settings should be left at their defaults unless you are experienced with communications and you know what alterations to make.

Options: The *Emulations* settings allow your computer to simulate types of terminal screens used for other communications systems, such as the French Minitel. Leave the setting at *Auto Detect* to ensure that HyperTerminal will pick the type of emulation that is best suited to the connections you make. The *ASCII* options refer to text that you will send and receive (as distinct from program files). The only default is to wrap any line of text that exceeds the window width, and you should retain this option. The other options are used only if you have problems with text. Looking at received text first, you will need to append line feeds only if you find that each incoming paragraph is received as a single line. You will need to force incoming text to 7-bit ASCII only if the text contains a lot of strange characters.

The *Sending* options are for sending line feeds, seldom needed, and for echoing the characters you type on the keyboard, which is needed only if you do not see them as you type them. The other name for this is *local echo*. When you have finished setting options you can connect. You will hear the modem dialling, some tones as the Bulletin board replies, a burst of noise, and then the sign-on message from the Bulletin board.

From then on, how you proceed depends on how you want to use the facilities of the bulletin board, which has nothing to do with HyperTerminal. The screen will show you what keys have to be pressed to obtain various facilities, and you can type messages to the Sysop (bulletin board system operator), look at files, download software and so on.

Disconnect: Click on the disconnect icon to stop the action if, for example, you have connected at an expensive time or if you simply wanted to check that your settings were correct. When you know that settings are correct you should use the *Save* item on the *File* menu of HyperTerminal to save your session file so that you can make use of it again without the need to enter numbers and options. This ensures that you need set up for a particular contact once only.

Transferring program and data files: Program and data files need to use a software system that checks each transmitted byte for accuracy. The default system for HyperTerminal is called *Zmodem*. You have a choice of these protocols as they are called, and in addition to Zmodem you can use systems called 1K Xmodem, Xmodem, Ymodem, Ymodem-G, and Kermit. A few connections, mainly Universities, may require you to use Kermit; most will accept Xmodem or Zmodem.

These systems can be made to perform with 100% reliability – either all of the codes will be received perfectly, or they will all be rejected because of errors. Methods of this type allow for several re-tries before they give up, so that some momentary interference does not stop a transmission, it only delays it.

Sending a file: When you click on the *Send File* option, you will see a form appear which asks you for a file name and you can also select your protocol type with the default of Zmodem. You can fill in the name with a filename that you know (with path), or you can use the *Browse* button to locate and select a file. When the *Send* button becomes active you can click it to send your file to the remote computer.

Receiving a file: The receive option also provides for a choice of protocols, and you can select a folder to receive the file. The default here is the *HyperTerminal* folder, but you can set up a folder for each particular connection if you want. While a file is being received using Zmodem you will see the Zmodem form.

When you send data you should always prepare it as a file before you use HyperTerminal. Remember that the telephone charges are ticking away all the time you are on line, so typing more than a few words while you are connected can be a costly business.

You can also opt to have received files sent to the printer. This does not slow down the transfer because the file is stored until printing is finished and HyperTerminal is released as soon as the file has been received – you do not need to wait until the printer has completed its work.

Note: Windows 95 regards HyperTerminal as a program for communicating with computers that are **not** running Windows, such as for links with Bulletin Boards that might use different types of computers. If you are communicating with a computer that is running Windows 95 you are advised to use the Dial-Up Networking action rather than HyperTerminal. This is a matter of taste – you might not want to use the complications of Dial-Up Networking or you might not have space for the extra files that it uses. HyperTerminal can communicate with any computer that is connected online, whether it runs Windows or not, and you need Dial-up Networking only if you want the ability to work as if you were networked to the other computer.

Icons

General: Each file, as seen in Explorer, carries an icon. In some cases, particularly for older MS-DOS programs, the icons for different programs are identical, but icons for Windows programs are usually distinctive. Icons for MS-DOS program files can be changed if required, but this action is not necessarily available for document files (unless you use a different method), nor for most Windows programs unless the manufacturer has provided for a choice. You **can**, however, always change the icon that is used for a shortcut.

Icon Size: You can alter the size of icons used in an Explorer display. With Explorer running, select *View* and then *Large Icons* or *Small Icons*. This does not permit you to alter the size of a single selected icon. You can also change the icon sizes that are used in the Start menu. Click Start — Settings — Taskbar and look for the checkbox marked *Show Small Icons in Start Menu*. Tick this box for small icons, and leave it unticked for larger icons.

Icons

Change program/shortcut Icon: With an MS-DOS program file, or a shortcut, selected in the Explorer display, click on File — Properties — Program — Change Icon. You will see a set of (typically 38) icons in a display that can be scrolled sideways. For some Windows programs, the set of available icons may be limited or there will be no *Change Icon* button in the *Properties* panel. Typically you will find a very limited choice for shortcuts, and no *Change Icon* button for most Windows programs. You can use the *Browse* button if it is present to find a larger range of icons, notably in the C:\WINDOWS folder, where you can browse the MORICONS.DLL file. Set the *Browse* action *Files of Type* box to *Libraries* so that you can find the DLL files more easily. Another set of icons is contained in WINDOWS\SYSTEM\SHELL32.DLL and yet more in MORICONS.DLL (also in the System folder).

Change document icon: On the Explorer display, click View — Options and click on the *File Types* tab. The display shows the registered document file types with icons and extension letters. Click on a file type, and then on the *Edit* button. You will now see a *Change Icon* button, and you can change to any other icon that is displayed, or browse for one of the libraries that contains more icons.

Desktop Icons: Open Control Panel either from Explorer or from Start — Settings. Double-click on *Display*, and select the *Appearance* tab. Open out the *Item* display so that you can see the entries *Icon, Icon Spacing (Horizontal)* and *Icon Spacing (Vertical)*. These settings can be changed to alter the size and spacing of the Desktop icons – they have no effect on other icons.

Notes: The default icons should be used unless you find that two programs are using very similar icons.

Installing W'95 components

General: When Windows 95 is installed, many users opt for a 'typical' installation or possibly a minimal installation rather than the full installation of all possible components. In particular, if Windows 95 has been installed on a machine with limited (less than 512 Mbyte) hard drive space, the 'typical' set of components will have been installed. Similarly, on a machine with less than 6 Mbyte of memory, a restricted version of Windows is installed, see the Notes below. You can, however, install other parts of Windows later without disturbing the settings you have made. See the entry for **Extract** for adding components which have been deleted and which cannot be selected in the way noted below.

Using Setup: Close all running programs other than Explorer. Start Control Panel from Explorer or from Start — Settings. Double-click on *Add/Remove Programs*, and when the panel appears, click on the tab marked *Windows Setup*. You will see a list of Windows components arranged in groups. Click on a group and then on the *Details* button to see the list of individual programs in the group. You can opt to select the whole group (black tick against the group name) or individual programs (black tick against selected programs, black tick on greyed background against the group). Click the *OK* button to get from a *Detail* display to the overall display, and click the *OK* button on the main display to start installation, which will require the Windows 95 CD-ROM or the floppy set to be inserted.

You can also remove components in this way, clicking to remove the tick from programs or groups that were originally ticked. This is preferable to deleting the files using Explorer because you may be able to identify the main EXE files of a program but you cannot be sure that you can find the DLL and other associated files.

Keyboard

Notes: Do **not** delete any DLL file in an Explorer display unless you are absolutely certain that it is redundant, because many DLL files are shared by more than one program.

• If you originally installed Windows 95 in a machine with less than 6 Mbyte of RAM, you should re-install Windows 95 completely if you subsequently expand the RAM to 8 Mbyte or more.

Keyboard

General: The keyboard that is connected to your computer will normally be the one intended for UK use, but some bargain-offer computers come with a US keyboard which will have no £ sign, and with the positions of some characters, notably inverted commas, altered. You can opt to use any language with your standard keyboard, and other types of keyboards, including the Microsoft Natural Keyboard, are available. If you want to plug in and use a different keyboard, see the entry for **hardware.** A wide range of options can be used to alter the behaviour of your keyboard without altering the hardware itself.

Change key actions: Start Control Panel either from Explorer or from Start — Settings. Double-click on *Keyboard* to see the 3-tab panel. The first tab is labelled *Speed*, and concerns the repeat action. You can alter the delay period between pressing down a key and starting the repeat action, and you can alter the rate at which a character repeats once the repeat action starts. If you have been used to a manual non-electric typewriter you might want to opt for a long delay and a slow repetition rate, because you may have acquired the bad habit of pausing with a key held down. If you are accustomed to a computer keyboard, you are more likely to want to use a short delay and a fast repetition rate.

- You can also change the cursor blink speed in this panel. Choose a rate which is fast enough for you to see that the cursor is blinking, but not so fast that it becomes hypnotic.

The second tab is labelled *Language* and it allows you to select the language that you want to use from your keyboard. There is a wide choice of languages available when you click the *Add* button, and you can select one or more to be made available. If you want another language to be the default, you can click the *Set as Default* button. You can also use the option buttons at the bottom of the panel to set a method of changing language, either with Left-Alt and Shift, Ctrl and Shift, or without any key method of changing language. Tick the box to make the language setting appear on the Windows 95 Taskbar. For a selected language, you can click the *Properties* button to see what type of keyboard is normally used for that language. The keyboard set that can be accommodated is:

Belgian   British   Canadian Multilingual   Danish   Finnish

French   French Canadian   German (IBM)

German (Standard)   Icelandic   Irish   Italian

Italian 142   Latin American   Norwegian

Portuguese (Brazilian ABNT2)

Portuguese (Brazilian Standard)   Spanish   Swedish

Swiss French   Swiss German   United States

US (Dvorak)   US (International)

Note that this is not exactly the same set of languages as are available from the *Language* selection list.

The third tab of this set is labelled *General*, and indicates the type of hardware keyboard that is in use (and which was originally installed when Windows was installed). This can be changed by clicking on the *Change* button, and you can use the *Show All Devices* button to indicate what types of keyboards (mostly older types) that can be used with the drivers that exist. If you want to use a new type of keyboard, you should have a suitable driver on a disc supplied by the manufacturer and you can click the *Have Disc* button to carry out the installation, then make that driver the default.

• You can also change the driver file for your keyboard by starting Control Panel and double-clicking on *System*, followed by *Device Manager*, *Keyboard*, and the keyboard type you are using.

Modifying action: The keyboard action can be modified, particularly by using the Accessibility options of Windows 95 (to add these options, see the entry for **Installing W95 components**). See the entry for **Accessibility** for details.

Notes: If you set your keyboard for another language and switch to that language you will not be able to use tools such as the spellcheck action of Word unless you have installed a dictionary file for that language.

• If your physical (hardware) keyboard is not suited to the language you will have problems with characters that are specific to that language.

. . . .

Media Player

General: Media Player is used along with coded sound or video data, and is useful if you intend to make use of multimedia. Your computer should contain a sound card, correctly installed. For animated video using larger window sizes, you may need a specialised video card, but in general you cannot expect the standard of video replay that you can obtain from a TV receiver and video recorder. The files for Media Player are held in the Windows\Media folder, and you may have deleted them (particularly the large AVI files) so as to save hard drive space. You can reinstate these files by using Setup again, see the entry for **Installing Windows 95 components**. You do **not** need to use Media Player separately if you are using a multi-media program such as Encarta from a CD-ROM.

Media Player files: Click Start — Programs — Accessories — Multimedia — Media Player. If you frequently want to use Media Player, make a shortcut to it in the Start menu. You can place the shortcut in the *Startup* folder if you want to use Media Player each time you start Windows 95. When the panel appears, click *Device*, which will list *CD Audio*, *Microsoft Multimedia Movie Play (MMM files)*, *Video for Windows (AVI files)*, *MIDI sequencer (MID or RMI files)* and *Sound (WAV files)*, all located in the WINDOWS\MEDIA folder. You can change to another folder if you know that you have suitable files in other folders.

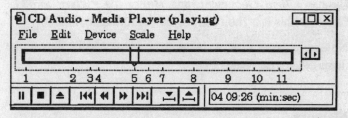

Starting play: With an appropriate file loaded, use the Media Player controls which are illustrated here for a music CD. The pointer has been placed on the CD track to be played, and the *Play* symbol clicked. The illustration shows the actions corresponding to the symbols, which are the standard symbols used on video recorders. The less-familiar symbols are for moving to a selection mark (earlier or later in the file)

and for creating these start and stop selection marks. These features are used if you want to be able to go to a portion of the file quickly and in particular if you want to repeat a portion of a file.

- You can simplify the Player display, which is particularly useful for CD play. Double-click on the title bar so that the display changes to one of tracks only, with a *Play* and a *Stop* symbol. You can double-click on the title bar again to restore the original panel.

- Remember that if your only use of Media Player is to play audio CDs, you should use CD Player instead, and set it up so that playing is automatically started when the CD is inserted, see the entry for **CD Player**.

Options: The Edit — Options menu content varies according to what type of multimedia object is being edited. For an Audio CD, for example, you can opt for *Auto Rewind* and *Auto Repeat*. The *OLE Object* section is used for all suitable objects, and there are selection boxes (taking the Audio CD object again as an example) for *Control bar on Playback*, *Play in Client Document*, and *Dither the Picture to VGA Colours* (this last choice is greyed out for an audio CD).

Notes: In general, it is better to reserve Media Player for items other than Audio CD.

- -

Memory

General: Memory, both the amount and the way in which it is used, is very important to the running of Windows 95. If you have insufficient memory then many actions, particularly when you are running large programs like Word-7 or switching between several programs, will be very slow. Windows 95 needs **at least** 8 Mbyte (and a reduced version of W95 will be installed if your computer contains significantly less than this). Speed is very noticeably improved when you upgrade to 12 Mbyte, and there is another improvement, not so great, when you upgrade from 12 Mbyte to 16 Mbyte. If your computer is a Pentium type, you must upgrade with SIMM memory strips installed in matching pairs, but the older 486 machines will usually accept an upgrade using a single SIMM.

Installing memory: Memory is installed by inserting SIMM units, usually of 4 Mbyte or more each, into the memory slots. The usual method is to slide the SIMM into its holder with the memory unit held at an angle, and then rotate the whole set until the SIMM clicks into place. There are books devoted to upgrading which illustrate the method in detail. No other action is needed – after the memory has been clipped into place, the computer will recognise the memory when it is switched on, and Windows 95 will make use of it.

Optimising use: It is possible to have adequate memory but make inefficient use of it. Open Control Panel from Explorer or from Start — Settings and double-click *System*. Click the *Performance* tab of the panel, and then click the *Virtual Memory* tab. You will see that the default option is in use, marked as *Let Windows manage my virtual memory settings (recommended)*. This is good advice, but if you have adequate hard drive space and you are not using DriveSpace on the hard drive, you can often achieve better performance by using the other option, *Let me manage my own virtual memory settings*. Click this option, and specify a minimum setting of 32 Mbyte and a maximum of 100 Mbyte (if your hard drive space permits). Do not tick the box marked *Disable Virtual memory* unless you have a very large memory size, 64 Mbyte or more.

Notes: If you find that switching from one program to another is very slow, with the hard drive working hard, this

Mouse

indicates that your memory is inadequate or that it is being badly used. If you have adequate memory, try saving your data and re-starting Windows. If this improves matters, the fault has been due to a program grabbing memory and refusing to release it.

Mouse

General: Unless you are using the **Accessibility options** for mouseless control, Windows 95 demands the use of a mouse. The mouse that was connected to your computer when Windows 95 was installed will be set up correctly, but if you change to another mouse type you will have to use the *Add New Hardware* option of Control Panel (see the **Hardware** entry). You can change many aspects of mouse use, such as the double-click speed and the pointer appearance.

Settings: Open Control Panel from Explorer or from Start — Settings. Double-click on mouse to show the *Settings* panel with its four tabs. The first tab covers button use. You can set up the mouse for right-handed or left-handed use, but do not assume that if you are left-handed it is better to reverse the mouse buttons. Try it for yourself and see if you prefer it. The other part of this panel controls the double-click speed, allowing you to move the slider until your favourite speed of double-clicking will operate the test item, a jack-in-the-box. You can click the *Apply* button to make a change and stay with the panel, or *OK* to make the change and return to Control Panel.

The second tab is marked *Pointers*. The main display shows the pointers that are currently in use for various Windows 95 actions. You can opt to use a *Scheme*, meaning a preset group of pointers, by clicking the arrowhead on this box. The default is usually *None* or *Windows Standard*, with the options of *3D Pointers*, *Animated Hourglasses*, *Windows*

MS-DOS programs

Standard (Extra Large) and *Windows Standard (Large)*. If you are worried about the speed of your computer, avoid the 3D and animated effects because they require more work from the processor. The **Microsoft Plus!** program contains additional animated pointers. You can also select from three sizes for each individual pointer, using the *Browse* button. In this way, you can make up a scheme of your own, using the *Save As* button to preserve your scheme for posterity. You can also, if you want, delete an added scheme.

The third tab is for *Motion*. You can set the speed at any position between *Slow* and *Fast*, and the *Fast* setting is usually preferable for many users. You can also opt to show pointer trails (mouse-tails) which are useful for portable machines with LCD screens (making the pointer movement visible), but not needed on a desktop with a cathode-ray tube monitor. The duration of trails can also be set. Try it for yourself to see if you like a pointer that leaves a trail.

The last tab is *General*, and is used only when you need to change the type of mouse.

Notes: You should take some time over the settings of such items as double-click speed, because if the settings match your normal use of the mouse you will be able to work faster because you will seldom need to repeat a double-click action.

MS-DOS programs

General: MS-DOS programs are older programs, many of them written long before Windows became established (though Windows 95 makes use of the MS-DOS operating system and is in that sense itself an MS-DOS program). These programs can run on the oldest types of PC, allowing only a maximum of 640 Kbyte of RAM, and though most of them can be run inside a window, a few can be used only

MS-DOS programs

after quitting Windows altogether. Those that can be used inside a window allow cut, copy and paste actions between the MS-DOS program and any Windows program. Nowadays, you are likely to use only a few utilities that demand MS-DOS. If you are using MS-DOS programs, you need to know how to use the MS-DOS system, and if you are not acquainted with the commands and the way they have to be entered you should consult a good book on MS-DOS such as *BP341 MS-DOS 6 explained*. Note that MS-DOS programs which are capable of altering memory content will usually have to be run by closing down Windows, see later.

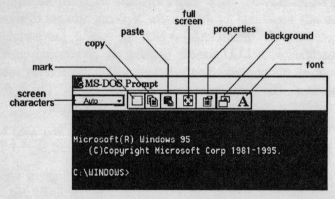

MS-DOS Prompt: Click Start — Programs — MS-DOS Prompt. When the MS-DOS window appears, start your MS-DOS program by typing its filename (and full folder path, if it is not in the C:\WINDOWS folder), or alternatively use the CD command to move to the correct folder and then type the program name. All commands are executed when you press the RETURN or ENTER key. Most MS-DOS programs (see below for exceptions) will run in this way and you can switch between the MS-DOS program and Windows programs as if the MS-DOS program were a Windows program. You can move and resize the MS-DOS window, and the icons, illustrated here, allow for some useful actions. When you are finished with the MS-DOS program, you can type the command EXIT (and press RETURN) to close the MS-DOS prompt window and return to Windows.

Program options: If an MS-DOS program runs without any apparent problems, you need not worry about the options that appear when you click File — Properties — Program with an MS-DOS program selected in the Explorer display. These are summarised here.

The *Tab* set for an MS-DOS program consists of *General*, *Program*, *Font*, *Memory*, *Screen* and *Misc*. The *General* panel follows the same pattern as for *Folders* or other files. The *Program* panel contains the icon and name of the program, and boxes labelled *Command Line*, *Working Folder*, *Batch File*, *Shortcut Key*, and *Run*. The *Command Line* shows the MS-DOS command that is used to start the program when it is run under MS-DOS. The *Working* (Folder) box shows where the program is located. The *Batch File* entry is seldom used; it can be used to contain the name of a batch file that will be run when this program is started. If a *Shortcut* key (or *hot key*) has been assigned, it will be shown in the next box, and the *Run* box allows you to specify if a program is run full-screen or in a reduced window. This last option is often unavailable and greyed out. The Panel contains an *Advanced* button and a *Change Icon* button (whose action is similar to that of changing the icon for any other file).

The *Advanced* button allows fine-tuning of the way that an MS-DOS program is run. The check boxes are labelled *Prevent MS-DOS Programs from Detecting Windows*, *Suggest MS-DOS Mode as Necessary*, *MS-DOS Mode*, and *Warn before entering MS-DOS Mode*. The *Prevent MS-DOS Programs from Detecting Windows* box can be ticked if the MS-DOS program is one of a small number that normally refuse to run if Windows is detected. *The Suggest MS-DOS*

MS-DOS programs

Mode as Necessary box should be ticked, because it allows Windows to decide what needs to be done, and this is always much faster than manual methods. The *MS-DOS Mode* box must be ticked if the program requires all other programs (including Windows) to be shut down before it can be run. If this is done, Windows will restart automatically when the MS-DOS program ends. The last box can be ticked to provide a warning before Windows is closed down.

The options concern the MS-DOS configuration, which is set by the files CONFIG.SYS and AUTOEXEC.BAT. The default is to use the CONFIG.SYS and AUTOEXEC.BAT files that run before Windows is started, but you can opt to specify different versions of these files which can then be edited in the two panels that are provided. A *Configuration* button can be clicked to ensure that a set of options is used each time this program is started.

• Do not alter the MS-DOS settings unless you know what you are doing. Consult the book *BP341 MS-DOS 6 Explained* if you need a tutorial on the use of MS-DOS. If you do not use any MS-DOS programs, or if the few that you use run without problems, you can ignore these settings.

The *Font, Memory, Screen* and *Misc.* Tabs will not necessarily contain any options unless the program is one that can make use of such options. The *Font* panel allows you to opt for *Bitmap Fonts Only*, *TrueType Fonts Only*, or *Both Font Types* (the default). You can select font size ranging from 2×4 (pixels) to 12×22, and panels show a *Window Preview* and a *Font Preview*. The *Panel* buttons are *OK*, *Cancel* and *Apply*. The *Apply* button will save the changes you have made without leaving the panel.

The *Memory* panel should not be changed unless you know what you are doing. The *Conventional Memory* section

94

allows amounts of *Total Memory* (in the first 640 Kbyte) to be selected, and also the *Initial Environment* memory. The default is to use *Auto*, but you can click the arrowhead to select various amounts of memory from 40 Kbyte upwards. The *Expanded (EMS) Memory* section is valid only if your computer uses EMS memory, unusual nowadays. The *Details* button can be click to show how to enable this type of memory, which is used only for a few older MS-DOS programs – such programs have now been superseded by Windows versions. The *Extended (XMS) Memory* section will, by default use the *Auto* setting for *Total Memory*, and will have the *HMA* (High Memory Area) box ticked. The last section deals with *MS-DOS Protected Memory (DPMI)* and once again, the *Auto* setting should be used unless you know that some other setting is appropriate. The *Panel* contains *OK*, *Cancel* and *Apply* buttons with the usual meanings.

The *Screen* panel is divided into sections marked *Usage*, *Window* and *Performance*. In the *Usage* section you can opt for *Full Screen* use or a reduced *Window* (the default). The *Initial* setting can be *Default* or you can opt for 25, 43 or 50 line display. The *Window* section has check boxes, ticked by default, for *Display Toolbar* and *Restore Settings on Startup*. These provide, respectively, for a Toolbar to be shown on an MS-DOS window and for the Window settings to be restored when you leave the MS-DOS program. The *Performance* set has boxes ticked for *Fast ROM Emulation* and for *Dynamic Memory Allocation*. If you experience display problems with the MS-DOS program, try removing the tick from the *Fast ROM Emulation* box. If the MS-DOS program must be given priority in memory allocation (which is unusual) remove the tick from the *Dynamic Memory Allocation* box.

The Misc. set contains a number of check boxes whose default values should not be changed unless you know that

MS-DOS programs

they ought to be changed. The *Foreground* item is *Allow Screen Saver*, and can be ticked if you want a Windows screen saver to be used on the MS-DOS Window. The *Mouse* items are *Quick Edit* and *Exclusive Use*. Ticking *Quick Edit* allows you to Cut and Copy by marking with the mouse, as you would for a Windows program. If this box is not ticked, you have to use the Edit — Mark menu item to select text for Cut or Copy actions. The *Exclusive Use* box will allow only the MS-DOS program to use the mouse, so that you will have no mouse pointer in Windows.

The *Background* section contains the *Always Suspend* box, which can be ticked to ensure that the program uses no system resources when it is inactive. The *Termination* section contains *Warn if Still Active*, which will issue a warning if you try to leave a program which is still running. The *Idle Sensitivity* setting can be left at its middle setting, but you can set it to *High* if you want the processor to ignore the program while it is idle, or to *Low* if you want the processor to pay more attention to an idle program.

The *Other* setting is for *Fast Pasting*, which should be ticked by default, though not all programs will allow this action. The last section deals with key combinations (hot keys) which will carry out Windows actions. If the MS-DOS program uses one or more of these key actions, you should remove the tick from the appropriate box or boxes. This will allow the use of that key combination in the MS-DOS program rather than having its normal Windows effect.

Awkward programs: A few MS-DOS programs cannot run normally when Windows is working, and have to be run either before Windows is loaded or after Windows has been closed. If you need to run an MS-DOS program of this type (usually programs which modify memory or hard drive contents), you can use one of the following routines.

Multimedia

When you switch on the computer, wait for the Windows 95 message, and then press the F8 key. When the menu appears, select *Command Prompt Only*, which will allow you to use MS-DOS (unless your old MS-DOS AUTOEXEC.BAT file contains as its last command the word WIN, which will start Windows). You can leave MS-DOS by typing WIN (and pressing the RETURN key) or restart the computer to enter Windows in a more orderly way.

The other option to run MS-DOS by itself occurs when you shut down, when you are given the option to *Restart the Computer in MS-DOS Mode*. This also allows you the use of MS-DOS exclusively, and you need to restart the computer when you are finished with the MS-DOS program(s) or type WIN (then press the RETURN key) to move to Windows 95.

Notes: There are various options on using specific CONFIG.SYS and/or AUTOEXEC.BAT files for specific MS-DOS programs, but you need some experience and expertise with MS-DOS to be able to use these options, and with the relentless march of Windows there is little point now that all the major programs you are likely to use exist in Windows versions.

Multimedia

General: The multimedia options are designed to allow you to make the most of whatever multimedia devices you have, though if you are only concerned with using software such as *Encarta* you can disregard almost everything except the volume control. Some of the settings, such as for sound recording quality or work with MIDI devices require knowledge and experience that is outside the realms of computing, and no attempt is made here, because of pressure of space, to explain such items. In general, if you don't understand the use of some option you probably don't need it!

Multimedia

Selecting options: Click on Control Panel from Explorer or use Start — Settings — Control Panel. Double-click the *Multimedia* icon. The panel which appears has five tabs which are explained below. These are labelled *Audio*, *Video*, *MIDI*, *CD Music*, and *Advanced*.

Audio tab: This consists of two sections. The *Playback* section deals with the playback of sound, and you can set the playback volume on a slider control, dragging the slider between *Low* and *High*. The *Preferred Device* that appears will correspond to your sound card – for example, SB16 Wave Out (220) refers to a 16-bit Sound Blaster card. Though there is an arrowhead on this option, the alternative that appears is usually *None*, since few stand-alone computers will have a choice of sound cards. The important selection box is labelled *Show Volume Control on the Taskbar*, and it allows the volume control to be operated by double-clicking an icon on the Taskbar rather than by using this panel.

The *Recording* section of this tab is similarly arranged with a *Volume Control* and a *Preferred Device*. The *Preferred Device* will be the *Wave In* section of the sound card, so that for the same Sound Blaster card it would read *SB16 Wave In (220)*. In addition, there is a *Preferred Quality* box, with the default *Radio Quality* selected. The arrowhead allows the options of *Telephone Quality* (suitable for voice-only recordings and using less disc space) and *CD Quality* (allowing high-quality recording of music, but requiring a large amount of disc space). If you are using a microphone for making recordings, choose *Telephone Quality* or *Radio Quality*.

The selection box in this section is labelled *Use Preferred Devices Only* and can be ticked if you have programs that demand a particular type of sound card which you have selected as the preferred device.

Video: The *Video* tab is fairly straightforward. You can opt to show a video display in a reduced *Window* or *Full Screen*. If you take the default option of a window, you have several choices on window size, with the default being original size. The other size options are *Double original*, $^1/_{16}$ *screen size*, $^1/_4$ *screen size*, $^1/_2$ *screen size* and *Maximised*. The defaults of *Window* and *Original* size are sensible, because unless you have a specialised video card which is capable of dealing with larger video images, attempts to show video pictures larger than original size will be very disappointing, with jerky movement and slow drawing of images. As Dr. Johnson said, "it is like a dog walking on its hind legs – it is not done well, but it is a wonder that it is done at all".

MIDI: This tab is of use only if you are using a MIDI interface to an electronic instrument, and if you know how to use it. If you need information on MIDI, see any of the excellent books on the subject by R. A. Penfold. The default setting is for a single instrument, using *MIDI for Internal OPL2/OPL3 FM Synthesis*, with an option of *MIDI for External MIDI Port*. You can also make a *Custom MIDI Configuration*, setting up a *MIDI scheme* of your own by way of the *Configure* button. There is also an *Add New Instrument* button which leads to a Wizard for installing new hardware.

CD Music: This tab is also simple, with a confirmation of the *CD-ROM drive letter* (usually D unless you have a second hard drive or a network), and a *Volume Control* setting for use with headphones (plugged into the headphone socket of the CD-ROM drive).

Advanced: This tab leads to a display of drivers, a portion of the display that is available from the System icon in Control Panel. In general, the settings will have been made on installation, and should not be changed unless you know that there are problems with a setting.

My Computer

- See the entry for **Volume Control** for details of setting up and using this facility.

Notes: Most of the tabs in the Multimedia section are concerned with specialised actions such as might be required for video or music editing or music synthesis, and only the volume control is of much applicability to the non-specialised user.

- -

My Computer

General: The *My Computer* display is an overall view of the main sections of the computer, meaning the drives (hard, floppy and CD-ROM), the Control Panel and the printers. It is a useful way of gaining access to drive information, formatting floppies, using Control Panel, etc., and because *My Computer* is really a format of Explorer, you can alter the display so that it is the same as that of Explorer, making it unnecessary to use both. You can also make a shortcut to *My Computer* on the Taskbar rather than have to minimise programs to use the shortcut on the Desktop.

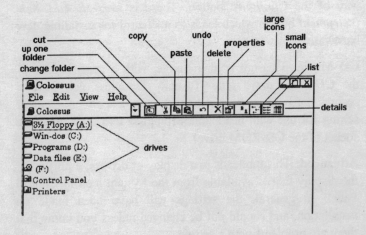

Starting: Reduce the size of any windows that are covering the Desktop and double-click the *My Computer* icon. You can *Minimise all Windows* by clicking the right-hand mouse button on any vacant portion of the Taskbar and selecting this option. The default *My Computer* display is a small window showing icons for all the drives, Control Panel, and Printers. The window has a menu, many of whose actions are also available from a toolbar, see illustration.

Another option for opening *My Computer* is to click with the right-hand mouse button on the icon to see the Quick Menu, and then on *Open*. If you click on *Explore* rather than on *Open*, you will see the *My Computer* information arranged in the Explorer way, and this latter view can also be obtained by holding down the Shift key and double-clicking the icon. You can also opt to make this the default view, dispensing with the need to use Explorer separately (see below).

- The advantage of using the Explorer type of View is that it has a *Tools* menu with *Find* and *Go To* actions, unlike the default menu of My Computer.

Display options: You can select display options either from the *View* menu or from the Toolbar. The Toolbar can be switched on or off from the *View* menu, and the other display options are *Status Bar*, *Large Icons*, *Small Icons*, *List*, and *Details*. Since the *My Computer* display is a variation on Explorer, the menu pattern is that of Explorer and the explanations will not be repeated here.

Renaming: If you think that the title *My Computer* is a trifle tacky, you can edit the name in the usual way – click on it twice (not in quick succession) and then edit. You might like to change the name to *Computer* or the actual model name of your computer. Note that you **cannot** rename the Recycle Bin, which is the other main Desktop icon.

Disc drives: You can click on any disc drive displayed in the

My Computer

My Computer view, so as to select it, and then on File — Properties or on the Properties icon in the Toolbar. Each drive is displayed as its reference letter (such as A:\, C:\) and any label name that has been assigned, see the entry for **Disc names**. The panel which appears shows the disc (for a floppy or CD-ROM) or drive (hard-drive) label name, and you can edit the name in its box. A pie-chart display shows the amounts of used and unused space, with colour codings that are explained. You can click on the *Tools* tab for a report on the three main disc checking actions of *Error checking*, *Backup*, and *Defragmentation*. For each of these headings, you will see a report on how many days have elapsed since the action was carried out, and a button that will start the action of error checking, backup or defragmentation respectively.

Other displays: You can use *My Computer* for quick access to Control Panel and Printer Control (which is normally through Control Panel). In each case, double-click to see an Explorer view of the Control Panel or the Printers. You can then double-click any Control Panel item to run it.

Explore view: You can use the *Options* menu of My Computer to make the Explorer view the default option. Click the View — Options button, then the *File Type* tab. In the list of File Types, move down to folder and click on that name, then on the *Edit* button. The box that appears will have the word **open** in bold print. If the word **explore** also appears, click on it and then on the *Set Default* button. If the word **explore** does not appear, click on the *New* button so that you can type the word **explore** and click the *Browse* button to find the Explorer program in the C:\WINDOWS folder. You can then leave this box so as to select the explore action and make it the default as above.

Other shortcuts: If you normally work with the Desktop

covered, it is very inconvenient to have to start *My Computer* by minimising all programs, though this can be done quickly by using the right-hand mouse menu. Another useful option is to place a shortcut to *My Computer* into the Start Menu set. To do this, use Explorer or the Explorer view of *My Computer*, so that the *My Computer* folder appears on the right hand side of the display. Click on it and then on File — Create Shortcut. Click on the shortcut so as to select it, and use Edit — Cut. Move to the folder in which you want to place the Shortcut and click the Edit — Paste option. You will see a *Shortcut to My Computer* item appear, allowing you to open *My Computer* from the Start menu.

Note: If you put a shortcut to *My Computer* in the *Startup* menu, you may find two copies when you next restart Windows. Like Explorer, *My Computer* will be automatically restored if it has been running when you switched down Windows, so that it is unnecessary to put it in the *Startup* menu unless you always close it before you switch down.

- -

Net Watcher

General: Net Watcher is used to check the resources that are available to you over a network, and is irrelevant if you are using a solo machine. This book excludes networking topics (which demand a large volume to themselves).

- -

Notepad

General: Notepad is a simple utility that is used to read, edit, or create ASCII document files of less than 64 Kbyte size. It is usually invoked automatically if you double-click on a file that carries the TXT extension letters, or it can be opened from the Start — Programs — Accessories menu. Notepad, as the name suggests, is also a convenient way of making

Notepad

short notes and saving them as a file or as a scrap (see entry for **scrap**).

Opening: Click Start — Programs — Accessories and click on the *Notepad* icon. If you make a shortcut in the Startup menu, you can have Notepad started for you automatically when you start Windows. See entry for **Taskbar**.

File menu: The File menu of Notepad consists of the usual *New*, *Open*, *Save* and *Save As* items. *Open* will start a search for files of type TXT, starting in the C:\WINDOWS folder, and with a brief Toolbar that allows you to move up one folder, create a new folder, display as a list or display with full details. You can type in a filename if you know what file you want, or opt in the *Files of Type* display for *All Files* rather than just text files – this is useful if you want to use Notepad to edit system files such as CONFIG.SYS or AUTOEXEC.BAT.

The *Save* item will save a file that has previously been opened and allocated a filename, and *Save As* allows you to specify a new name, new location or both, either for an existing file or for a piece of text that you have just created. You need not save a document file with the TXT extension, but using this default makes it much easier to locate such files when you later want to open them.

Edit menu: The Edit menu contains an *Undo* action which will undo the most recent action, but not a string of actions. The key alternative to the menu is Ctrl-Z. The familiar *Cut*, *Copy* and *Paste* actions are also in this menu. *Cut* (Ctrl-X) will remove selected text from Notepad, and *Copy* (Ctrl-C) will make a copy but not delete the original. *Paste* (Ctrl-V) will paste in cut or copied material (you can open more than one copy of Notepad and paste material from one to another). There is also a *Delete* item, but the use of the Delete key is usually more convenient.

Objects

The *Select All* item allows all of the text to be selected without the need to drag the cursor over all of the text, and the *Time/Date* option (F5 key) will place the current Time and Date information into your document at the cursor position. The *Word Wrap* option can be clicked to ensure that lines in Notepad are the same width as the window. You should always use this option when you are viewing files as otherwise you may need to scroll sideways to see the whole of a line. The option is also useful when you are typing because it prevents lines from disappearing beyond the right hand edge of the window.

Search: The *Search* menu item contains only *Find* and *Find Next* (with the F3 key options for *Find Next*). Clicking *Find* produces a small panel which you can use to specify a piece of text that you want to find in your Notepad file. When you have typed this text, another *Find Next* button in the panel is activated, and you can click it to carry out the *Find* action, and subsequent *Find Next* items. You can use the F3 key or the Search — Find Next options if you have closed the *Find* panel. The *Find* panel contains a check box for *Match Case*, and you can opt to search either up or down a document.

Notes: Though Notepad is a text editor, you can open files that are not text files. If you use it to open a program file, for example, you can read any text that is built into the program, and all the program codes will appear as various character shapes. Do not attempt to change and re-save any program file with Notepad, because this will almost certainly cripple the program unless you have edited only a portion of text, making changes that do not affect the number of characters in the text.

Objects

General: An *object* is an inserted item in a document, which

Objects

might be a piece of text from another document, an illustration from Paint or other drawing program, a burst of sound, an animation, a portion of a spreadsheet, or any other extracted material. An imported object can be embedded or linked into a document. When an object is embedded, it becomes a part of the document and is saved with the document. When the object has been created by a different type of program (as for a drawing embedded in a text document) it can be edited by double-clicking on the object. This will start the program which created the object, with the object in place to be edited. When an object is linked, its file is connected to your document, but only by a shortcut of a few bytes, so that the size of the document is almost unchanged. To edit the object, you need to run the program that created it, save the altered file, and update the links to your document (for example, use Format — Links in Word).

Embed object: The ordinary *Cut* or *Copy* and *Paste* action is an embedding action, and you can use this in the normal way. An object can be embedded in this way even if no file copy exists, and some programs, such as Word, allow you to create an object for embedding by starting up a suitable program from a Word instruction. An object can be embedded in more than one document (and into more than one place in a document).

Link object: If an object is to be linked, it must be created in a suitable program, and saved as a file. It can then be selected and *Cut* or *Copied*, and in the document, pasted in using the *Paste Special* command, and opting for *Paste Link*. If the document is created by a program that does not support linking (rare nowadays) there will be no *Paste Link* command. An object can be linked into more than one document and into more than one place in a document. If you subsequently change the file for the linked object, all the copies that appear in documents will also change. Programs that support linking will allow the editing of links, so that you can update links, or change links to another file.

Note: Different programs treat these actions differently, and you need to know what variations exist on your own software.

- You can embed or link an object inside another object. For example, in Word you can embed a drawing in a document and have an Equation embedded within the drawing.

- Remember that embedded objects can greatly increase the size of a file.

....

Paint

General: Paint is the Windows 95 graphics painting program that replaces the Paintbrush program of Windows 3.1. Many users prefer Paintbrush, particularly for its ability to create the compact PCX type of data files, and for better cursor control, and so use the older program rather than its replacement. Paint, like WordPad, is a fairly substantial program in its own right, and would require a book of about this size again for a really full treatment, so that what follows is only an outline guide.

Starting Paint: Click Start — Programs — Accessories — Paint. The Paint window will appear and should be maximised if you want to create a drawing. The icons are illustrated and named in the illustration.

Colours: Click on a colour from the palette using the left-hand mouse button to make this the foreground (drawing) colour. Click on a colour with the right-hand mouse button and then click on Image — Clear Image to make this the background colour. If you click a colour with the right-hand

Paint

mouse button and do not use the *Clear Image* command, this colour will be used only for filling closed shapes (*Fill colour*).

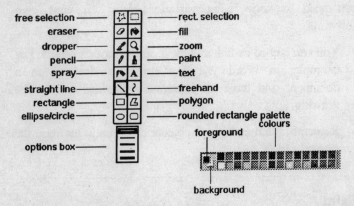

Drawing shapes: Click on the drawing tool and drag the cursor to draw the corresponding shape. The freehand line must be drawn with precise mouse movements, but other shapes can be controlled by using the Shift key. Drawing a straight line with the Shift key held down will make the line perfectly horizontal, vertical, or at 45°, depending on the direction of dragging. Drawing a rectangle with the Shift key held down will create a perfect square, and drawing an ellipse with the Shift key held down will draw a perfect circle.

You can draw a closed shape in outline, with a fill, or consisting of a fill only with no outline, according to your selection from the *options box* at the left-hand side. The same box will provide a set of line thickness options when a line tool is selected (and other options for other actions). If you want to draw a closed shape with a thick line boundary, select the line thickness *before* you select the closed shape tool. The paintbrush tool uses the options box to provide a set of brush shape and size options, and the spray-gun tool can use a set of spray patterns. The eraser options are for size, and the magnifier options are zoom sizes. Text and selection tools can use the options box to select positioning in front of other objects or behind them.

Selecting and altering: Any drawn shape can be selected using one or other of the selection tools. The rectangular selection tool allows you to draw a perfect rectangle around the area that you want to select, and carry out any permitted action on the enclosed area. The freehand selection tool allows you to define the shape of a selected object more closely as you drag the mouse, though the selection outline appears as a rectangle when you release the mouse button.

On a selected object, the actions that you can carry out are *Moving, Copying, Deleting, Flipping, Rotating, Stretching, Skewing* and *Colour Inversion*. Moving is done by dragging the selected area with the four-arrow icon visible. Copying can be done by dragging with the Ctrl key hold down or by using *Copy* and *Paste* from the Edit menu. Deleting requires you to press the Delete key, the Ctrl-X keys, or the Edit — Clear Selection menu action.

The other effects are reached either through the Image menu or by using Ctrl-key combinations. Image — Flip/Rotate (Ctrl-R) will produce a panel with the options of *Flip horizontally, Flip vertically,* or *Rotate,* with a choice of 90°, 180° and 270° angles. The *Stretch/Skew* menu choice (Ctrl-W) shows a panel with *Horizontal* and *Vertical* options for the *Stretch* action, each with a percentage panel into which you can enter the percentage stretch amount. The *Skew* portion of the panel allows for *Horizontal* or *Vertical* skew, with the amount specified in degrees. The *Invert Colour* choice (Ctrl-I) will reverse the foreground and background colours, and this action shows up very clearly the difference between a rectangular selection and a freehand selection.

The text tool allows text, with the usual options of fonts and sizes, to be added to a picture. If you click View — Text Toolbar you will see a toolbar appear that allows easy choice of *Font*, *Size*, and effects (*Bold*, *Italic* and *Underline*). When you click the *Text* tool, you can draw a *Text Box*, and when the cursor appears, you can type your text which will fill the box. You can edit the text or re-size the box until it fits your text, and then click outside the box to remove the box and leave the text. The text will appear either hiding the drawing under it or superimposed, depending on your setting of the *Options box* icons.

Measurements: Paint is not intended for making scale drawings, which is the task of a CAD program (try SmartSketch if you need precise drawings with none of the complications of a full-blown CAD program, or AutoSketch if you need full CAD facilities in a package that is compatible with AutoCAD but much easier to use). Measurements are indicated on the status bar of Paint, with the cursor position indicated in units of Pixels (*Pels*), and a box measurement indicator that show the size of a closed shape or selection box while you are drawing it (but not after you have released the mouse button). Note that though you can specify units in the Image — Attributes menu, only the pel units are shown on the status bar.

Colours: The basic colour palette of Paint contains 28 colours if you are using a 16-colour display (some 'colours' are patterns), and larger amounts if you are using a 256-colour (or higher) screen. You can use the Options — Edit Colors menu to select from a larger number (48 for the 16-colour screen) or to make your own (*Custom*) colours. Click on a colour in the *Palette*, then on Options — Edit Color. You can click on a colour in the larger colour box in this panel (then on the *OK* button) to place this colour into the *Palette*, replacing the original colour, or you can click the *Custom Color* button to create your own colour by clicking on the colour display that appears in an extension of the panel.

If you create *Custom Colors*, you can save your new colour set as a PAL (palette) file using Options — Save Colors, and you can subsequently load this or any other saved colour set by using the Options — Get Colors menu item. The last item in the *Options* menu is *Draw Opaque* which can be ticked to prevent a selected item showing any item that it covers. If the tick is removed, the underlying item becomes visible. This is the same action as is carried out by the icon pair in the options box when a selection action is being used.

File menu: The *File* menu of Paint contains the usual items of *New*, *Open*, *Save* and *Save As* which carry out the same actions as have been described for other programs. The Open command allows the choice for *Files of Type* of *Bitmap files* (the default), *Paintbrush files* (including PCX files) or *All Files* (which displays all files, but allows only compatible files to be opened). The *Save As* command allows the use of *Files of Type* consisting of *Monochrome Bitmap*, *16-colour Bitmap*, *256-colour Bitmap*, *24-bit Bitmap*, and *All files*. The *All Files* option allows you to use any extension letters you choose, but the file will be a bitmap file – you can, for example, create a file called TEST.PCX, but this will be a bitmap file, not a PCX type of file.

The second section of the *File* menu contains *Print Preview*, *Page Setup* and *Print*. The *Print Preview* produces (after some time) a view of the printed page with your drawing in place to show how the page will appear. If you have more than one drawing on separate pages you can use the *Next Page* and *Prev. Page* buttons to look at different drawings, also a *Two Page* option to see two pages on screen, and there is a *Print* button if you want to print without returning to the main menu. The *Page Setup* item will show a page diagram, with boxes for *Paper Size*, option buttons for *Orientation*

Paint

(*Portrait* or *Landscape*), and *Margins*, with a default value of 0.75" for *Left*, *Right*, *Top* and *Bottom* margin. The last item in this set is *Print*, which will print the drawing using the values in *Page Setup*.

The *Send* item of the *File* menu allows a drawing in Paint to be transmitted by E-mail or Fax, providing that you have set up *Microsoft Exchange*. Note that this is not the same as the Windows 95 *Send To* command which allows a file to be sent to a destination determined by the contents of a folder, see the **Send To** entry.

There are two *Set* items, labelled as *Set as Wallpaper (Tiled)* and *Set as Wallpaper (Centered)* which allow an image to be used as a Desktop wallpaper (see **Desktop** entry). These commands allow you to prepare Wallpaper of your own design.

Finally, the *File List* in the *File* menu is of recently-used files, allowing you to recall any of these files rapidly with a single click.

Edit menu: The Edit menu contains an *Undo* (Ctrl-Z) item, allowing you to reverse up to three of the most recent actions. There is also a *Repeat* (F4) item which will reverse an Undo. The usual set of *Cut* (Ctrl-X), *Copy* (Ctrl-C) and *Paste* (Ctrl-V) follow, and there are also the *Clear Selection* and *Select All* options.

The last two *Edit* menu items are particularly useful. *Copy To* allows a selected portion of an image to be saved to a file for which you can specify a filename and type, and a folder location. The other command, *Paste From*, carries out the opposite action of pasting an image from a file into a selection box that you can place anywhere on your page. You can, if you want, create the selection box first, but this will not alter the scale of the image so that it fills the box – the selection box will alter size so as to suit the image.

View menu: The View menu contains *Toolbox*, *Color Box*, *Status Bar*, *Zoom*, *View Bitmap* and *Text Toolbar*. The first three items are selected on (ticked) by default, but you can remove them if you prefer. Clicking on the *Zoom* item produces the choice of *Normal* (Ctrl-Page Up), *Large* (Ctrl-Page Down) or *Custom*, and the *Custom* item can be clicked to allow the selection of 100%, 200%, 400%, 600% or 800%. When a magnification of 400% or more is used, you can click *Show Grid* to display a grid that shows pixels, and you can then edit a shape one pixel at a time, or use the drawing tools on the enlarged view (which is often quicker). The other option in this set is *Show Thumbnail*, which shows a small copy of the main picture so that you can see the result of editing on pixels.

The *View Bitmap* item allows you to see your image uncluttered by toolbars, and clicking anywhere in the image area will return you to normal view. The last option is to turn the *Text Toolbar* on or off.

Image Attributes: The other *Image* menu items have already been mentioned. *Image Attributes* allows you to alter the size of the picture outline, the units in which this is stated, and the option of colour or monochrome. Altering size is one method of cropping an image, though it is not so useful as using *Copy To* (with an area selected) or the action of cropping in another document (such as a Word document). Your units choice is inches, centimetres or pels (pixels).

Notes: Unlike Paintbrush which allowed you to move a selection pixel by pixel using the cursor keys (with the mouse button held down), Paint has no way of allowing such precision of movement, and you should reduce the sensitivity of the mouse (using the Mouse item in Control Panel) if you want to carry out such actions.

- Unlike Paintbrush, Paint allows you to change *Image Attributes* without clearing the image.

113

Passwords

. . . .

Passwords

General: Passwords are used mainly by users of machines on a network, which is a set of topics that is not covered in this book. Solo users need not use passwords, and will find that all of the passwording options described in the Help pages are inapplicable when there is no network fitted. Where the use of a password is permitted with Windows 95 used alone, you should either ignore the provision, or use a password that you can remember but which no-one else can guess. One useful tip is to make a word out of the initial letters of a line of a poem or a song.

. . . .

Path

General: A path is a route to a file, described by starting at the drive and going through the folders and sub-folders until the folder holding the file is reached. Paths are particularly important when you are using MS-DOS commands, because the path to a file must be specified. Using Windows, you can browse for a file, eliminating the need to make a note of the path name.

Conventions: The drive letter is followed by a colon and a backslash, such as C:\. Each folder and subfolder is surrounded by a backslash. For an MOS-DOS path, no folder or file name can exceed eight characters (with an optional three-character extension on the filename), and the whole path cannot use more than 64 characters. For example, C:\WINDOWS\CURSORS\APPSTART.ANI is a path to an animated cursor called APPSTART which is in the CURSORS folder which in turn is in the WINDOWS folder on the C:\ drive.

Windows 95 files and folders can use spaces and long names that are forbidden for MS-DOS, and all paths that contain such names should be enclosed in quotes if you need to type the path. For example, "C:\My old files\old letters.doc" is an acceptable path for a Windows 95 file. Another convention is used when you type a path to a remote computer on a network, using two backslashes ahead of the computer name, and the normal path conventions following.

Notes: If you use the *Browse* button that is provided on most panels that require paths, you do not need to type any paths, only to click on the file in the display and then click the *Open* button.

. . . .

Performance

General: The performance of your computer is ultimately restricted by its microprocessor chip, amount of memory, hard disc size and organisation and other built-in factors, and there are several steps that you can take to ensure that your programs run as fast as is possible on your system.

Chip: If your computer uses a 486 chip, consider a Pentium upgrade. If it uses a Pentium chip, consider an upgraded faster Pentium. If it uses a 386 or earlier consider a new computer.

Memory: Your computer should be fitted with as much memory as you can afford. There is no substitute.

Hard drive: The hard drive should be a fast type, and of adequate size – the usual size at the time of writing is 850 Mbyte.

Organisation: see under the **memory** entry.

Phone Dialler

Phone Dialler

General: The Phone Dialler is a simple utility that provides the actions of a ten-memory telephone within Windows. You must have a modem connected to your computer and to the telephone lines.

Using: Start Phone Dialler from Start — Programs — Accessories and enter the number using the computer keys or by clicking the diagram of a telephone keypad. Make certain that the modem is switched on and when you have entered the number, click the *Dial* button. You will hear the dialling tones and a message will be shown when you can pick up the telephone and talk. You can click the *Hang Up* button to terminate the call, or put down the telephone.

Speed dial: You can enter names and numbers into a *Speed dial* list by clicking Edit — Speed dial. When you have done this, the names will appear on the *Speed dial* list in Dialler and you can dial by clicking on the name.

Dialling properties: Click Tools — Dialling properties to see the *Properties* panel. The first section deals with the location of your phone, and starts with *I am dialling from*, with a box containing the word *Home*. You can click the *New* button to fill in another description such as *Work* and place it into the *Dial from* list so that you can select when you dial. The following line contains *The area code is:* with a space for the area code that you use, and the third line for international calls is headed *I am in*, with a space which displays *United Kingdom (44)* and whose arrowhead can be clicked to display any country from *Afghanistan (93)* to *Zimbabwe (263)*.

The second section is headed *How I dial from this location*, and it deals with telephones which are part of a larger system. The first line is *To access an outside line, first dial:* with a space and the phrase *for local*. You can enter here a figure

116

such as 9 used to get an outside line from a private branch exchange system. A second portion of this line provides a space for an access code for long-distance dialling, if appropriate. There is a *Dial using Calling Card* space which can be used if your telephone can accept any of the card systems that are listed when you tick the *Change* button – British Telecom appears in this list in the UK version of Windows 95. Another line is headed *This location has call waiting. To disable it, dial*, and is followed by the choice of codes (click the arrowhead) of **70, 70#* or *1170*. Finally, there are option buttons for *Tone Dialling* (default) or *Pulse dialling*.

- It should not be strictly necessary to fill in any part of this panel, other than to make sure that the correct type of dialling is selected.

Connect Using: This part of the *Tools* menu is used to check that your modem is connected, and if Windows 95 has installed the modem correctly nothing needs to be done. The panel starts with a *Line* section which should display a Modem name (often *Standard modem* if a non-US manufacturer is unrecognised), and the arrowhead will not be useful unless you have more than one modem available and installed. The *Address* space will, by default, contain *Address 0* unless your phone system uses multiple lines (allowing you to click the arrowhead and select a line).

Note: The same dialling facility exists, with a much larger range of names and numbers useable, in the *Cardfile* utility that was part of Windows 3.1 and which is often present on a Windows 95 installation. Since Cardfile also allows for an address and notes, it is really a much more useful program.

Plug and Play hardware

Plug and Play hardware

General: Hardware additions to your computer should by now all be of the Plug and Play type, meaning that they contain stored information on installation that Windows 95 can act upon. This makes the installation of such hardware literally plug in and use, as distinct from the routine of adjusting jumpers and configuring software that was needed for older hardware.

Installation: With the computer switched off, connect the new hardware, making certain that all plugs are firmly inserted and, where appropriate, locked into place, and any inserted cards screwed down into position. Replace the covers on the machine (unless the hardware has been connected through a port), and switch on. When Windows is running, start Control Panel from Explorer or from Start — Settings, and double-click on *Add New Hardware*. Follow the instructions, allowing Windows to detect the new hardware automatically. See the **hardware (add)** entry for details

Notes: Older hardware may need driver software read from a floppy, but you should use the *Add New Hardware* routine and try for auto-detection before assuming that manual installation will be needed. Some older hardware still comes with instruction for installation under Windows 3.1, but it should be possible to make a satisfactory installation under Windows 95 – consult the hardware manufacturer if you are in doubt.

Plus!

General: Microsoft Plus! is a program, sold separately from Windows 95 or Microsoft Office, which contains some enhancement for Windows 95. Many of these are trivial (like animated cursors), but if you need to use compressed drives (see the entry in this book), the Plus! package contains *DriveSpace-3* which is a significant improvement on DriveSpace-2. Even if you do not wish to use compression, DriveSpace-3 can be used specifying 1:1 compression so that files are not compressed, but the problems of disc clusters are eliminated, allowing more disc space for short files.

Installation: Install Plus! using the Add/Remove Programs option from Control panel, and follow the guidance on the portions of Plus! that you want to use.

Notes: Plus! contains *System Agent*, which will check the condition of your computer at set intervals and run programs such as Defragmenter at these times. This automatic action can be useful if your computer is used intensively, but the automatic nature of these actions can be upsetting if you are in the middle of important work when a *System Agent* action starts.

Printing

General: The aim of creating documents is to print them, so that the setup and use of the printer is a very important part of Windows 95. Remember, however, that the program that you are running will to a considerable extent determine how you use the printer, and if you are running a DOS program it must contain its own printer drivers because DOS programs cannot make use of the Windows drivers. If you want to be able to use printers that are not connected to your system (either directly or mapped through a network) you can install such printers and opt to create a disc of printer codes so that your documents can be printed from this disc by using an MS-DOS command on another computer that is equipped with the desired printer.

Printers: Start Control Panel from Explorer or from Start —

Printing

Settings. Double-click on the *Printers* icon. The *Printers* window will open, showing in icon form all the printers (possible only one) that are installed on your system. As noted above, you may want to install some printers that are not available to your own system. To do this, double-click the *Add Printer* icon to start a Wizard which will take you through the necessary steps. When you come to specify a *Port*, use the *File:* option if you do not have the printer connected. The same Wizard is used if you want to change to another printer connected to your system, specifying the normal printer port *LPT1*.

Printer Setup: Programs that use the printer will all provide for setting up the printer for their own purposes, but the methods can vary. Some will provide a File — Printer Setup menu, others will allow *Setup* actions from File — Print. For example, *Word* uses File — Print to display a panel which has a *Properties* button for setting up the printer (as distinct from items such as page range, number of copies, etc.), and *Notepad* uses its *Page Setup*, again with a *Properties* button. A more extensive *Properties* panel is obtained by clicking File — Properties from the *Printers* window of *Control Panel*. This panel covers both text and graphics printing, and its tabs are described below.

The *General* tab shows the printer name, and has a space for any comment (such as the expected life of a toner or ink cartridge). You can also opt for a separator page with options of *None, Full* or *Simple*. The separator is a page that will be printed between documents and is useful if your printer is being used over a network or if you often print documents one after another. A *Full* separator page contains graphics and a *Simple* separator contains text only. You can also prepare a page for yourself (using WMF graphics images along with text), save it, and use the *Browse* button to establish it as a *Separator*.

The *Defaults* tab contains a large amount of controls that you normally need to set up only once (and you may not need to alter settings). *Print to the following Port* is usually set for port LPT1, and you can click the arrowhead if your printer is connected to another port (including FILE: or a serial port). There are buttons for *Add Port* and *Delete Port* (used mainly for network ports). The *Print using the following Driver* section should show the name of your default printer, and you can click the arrowhead to change to any other installed printer. There is a button for *New Driver* if you are updating a printer driver. Two more buttons are used for Network printers, labelled *Capture Printer* and *End Capture*. These are used so that you can ensure that you have uninterrupted use of a printer while you print your document, and then release the printer for other users. The *Timeout Settings* are used to avoid error warnings that can appear if the printer is not available. The *Not Selected* time is the time for which Windows will wait for the printer to become available when you start printing a document. You might want to set this to the time it takes for the printer to be ready after switching on. The *Transmission Retry* setting may need to be longer (I use 150 seconds), and it avoids an error message caused by the computer sending data faster than the printer can deal with it. Alter these settings as you need to, based on experience. The other two buttons, at the foot of the panel, are labelled *Spool Settings* and *Port Settings*; these are explained in the *Print Options* for this entry.

The *Paper* tab starts with a list of *Paper Sizes*, with the default size (usually A4 in the UK) selected. You can scroll the list sideways to see other acceptable sizes. *Orientation* can be set with option buttons as *Portrait* (default) or *Landscape*. You can set *Paper Source* if you are using a laser printer with multiple paper trays or cartridges, and also the *Number of Copies*. Click the button marked *Unprintable*

Printing

Area to see the minimum margins that your printer can use, in units of 0.001 inches or 0.01 mm. These margins are typically about 5 mm for laser printers. If you alter these settings, you can click the *Restore Defaults* button to replace them. The *About* button on the main tab panel will show the printer driver version number, and you can also use the main *Restore Defaults* button to make all settings the default values for your printer.

The *Graphics* tab determines how graphics will be printed, and this tab does not appear for programs that deal with text only. Do not alter these settings until you have had some experience with the graphics programs that you want to use. The *Resolution* setting will show the highest resolution that your printer can produce, and you may want to use a lower value, for example, because you are using ordinary paper with an ink-jet printer, or because you want to match screen resolution, or because your laser printer does not have enough memory for large high-resolution images. *Dithering* settings are provided for colour or grey-scale images, allowing intermediate colours to be produced by alternating dots of different colour, or grey shades to be produced by altering the spacing of black dots. You can opt for *None*, *Fine*, *Coarse*, *Line Art*, or *Error Diffusion*. The general rule is that if you are using resolution of 200 dots per inch or less, select *Fine*, if you are using resolution of 300 dots per inch or more, choose *Coarse* dithering. The *Line Art* setting can be used if all of your work consists of lines only with no colour or grey fillings, and you can opt for *Error Diffusion* if you are printing photographic images with no clear borders. You may need to experiment with the settings to find what is most appropriate for your own work. The *Intensity* control is set midway by default, and provides the overall value of light or shade for graphics. You can click on the *Restore Defaults* button if you have made alterations and want to get back to normal. Some graphics programs will make the optimum printer settings for you so that you do not need to use these options for yourself.

The *Fonts* tab allows you to select any font *Cartridges* that you are using in a printer. You are unlikely to need this because the use of Windows with TrueType fonts has superseded the need for expensive font cartridges. For printing with TrueType fonts you can use options that are described as *Download as Bitmap Soft Fonts* or *Print TrueType as Graphics*. The *Download* option is the (faster) default and should be used if your document consists mainly of text. If your document contains a a large number of graphics and if text is not extensively repeated, the *Graphics* option can be more useful. The *Graphics* option also allows graphics to be printed over text.

The *Device Options* tab applies mainly to laser printers with added memory. You can use this panel to notify the amount of memory in your laser printer and to determine how the memory will be used on a scale from *Conservatively* to *Aggressively*. Use the default settings for memory use unless you are experienced enough to know that you can benefit from altered settings.

Printing a document: You would normally print a document while you are using the program that created the document, but printing can also be carried out by using Windows 95 methods. For example, you can click with the right-hand mouse button on a document name (in an Explorer view) and then click on *Print*. The document will be opened using the program that created it and printed from that program (for example, a file with the DOC extension will be printed using Word). You can also click the file name with the left-hand mouse button and use the File — Print menu of Explorer, or you can use the *Send To* action of Explorer's *File* menu, with a shortcut to the printer. If you have a printer icon on the

Printing

Desktop, you can drag the filename to this icon to carry out the print action, or you can keep a shortcut to your printer in the same folder as your document files. These printing options all make use of the program that created the document file and are not intended to be used with a file that already contains printer codes (saved using a *Print to File* option). These need to be printed using the MS-DOS command COPY *filename* PRN because this prevents any other program from intervening.

Print status: Printing using Windows 95 is normally *spooled*, meaning that the printing codes produced by the program that is in control will be saved in memory and fed out to the printer as fast as the printer can cope with them. This prevents the computer from being tied up during a print run. You can carry out the Print action on a set of documents, which will form a print queue, and these will be dealt with in turn. During this time, a printer icon will appear on the Taskbar and you can double-click this icon or click on it with the right-hand mouse button to get a status report, showing which document is currently printing and what other documents are awaiting printing. You can see this *Status* window also by selecting your printer in the *Control Panel Printers* display, and clicking on File — Open.

- For documents that are not currently being printed, you can alter the order of printing by dragging a file to a different position in the print queue.

- The *Status* window is useful only for files that are being printed either locally or through a network, not for documents that are being printed to a file. If you have not opted for print spooling, no status window will appear.

The *Printer Status* display has a menu set of *Printer*, *Document*, *View*, and *Help*. The *Printer* set contains *Pause Printing*, to halt the printer action (local printer only) while you carry out some other task. This is useful if you find that your computer is responding only very slowly while a document is being printed – you can restore action by clicking again to remove the tick. You can also use *Purge Print Jobs* to remove all waiting documents from the print queue (if the printing of a document has started it will be completed). If you are not using your default printer, you can make this setting, and the *Properties* settings, also from the *Printer* menu.

The *Document* menu also contains *Pause Printing* and *Cancel Printing*, and the *View* menu allows you to turn the *Status* bar display of the Window on or off.

Print options: The most important printing option is the use of spooling, and this is set from the Properties — Details tab of the Printer item in Control Panel. Click the *Spool Settings* button in this panel to see the *Spooling* panel. The most important option is *Spool print jobs so that program finishes printing faster*, and if you click on the alternative of *Print directly to the Printer*, you will not be able to use the computer while the printer is working. If you use the default of spooling, you can choose when to start printing, either *After the last page has spooled* or (the default) *After the first page has spooled*. You can select the *Spool Data Format*, which by default is the format called *EMF*, but if this causes printing problems, the alternative of *RAW*, which is slower, can be used. For printers which use a moving printhead, you can enable or disable *Bi-directional Printing*. There is a *Restore Defaults* button at the foot of the panel in case you have lost track of the original settings.

The other button on the *Details* tab of Control Panel — Printers is labelled *Port Settings*. The options in this small sub-panel are to *Spool MS-DOS print jobs* and to *Check Port state before printing*. These should both normally be checked.

Recycle Bin

Notes: The Print Screen key, which for MS-DOS programs will print the screen image on paper, acts as a screen capture key in Windows 95, placing the image on the clipboard. You need to use a graphics program to paste the clipboard image in and to print it.

Recycle Bin

General: When you delete a file in the normal way, selecting a name or names and pressing the Delete key or using an Edit — Delete menu, the file is not removed from the disc, and its name and details are simply transferred to another folder labelled as the Recycle Bin. This folder can be accessed from any drive by way of shortcuts. When you empty the Recycle Bin, all of the files contained in the Bin are deleted (though if you have not saved any files subsequently, they may be recoverably by using MS-DOS recovery programs.

Full deletion: If you want to delete a selected file, or set of files, as distinct from using the Bin, press the Shift-Delete keys rather than the Delete key alone. In some circumstances, you will see a message about sending the file to the Recycle Bin, and you will need to click on the *No* button and use Shift-Delete again.

Emptying the bin: There are several methods. If the *Recycle Bin* icon is visible on the Desktop, click on the icon with the right-hand mouse button, and then on *Empty Recycle Bin*. You can also click on the *Recycle Bin* in an Explorer view of *any* hard drive, and then on File — Empty Recycle Bin.

• You can also remove files from the bin selectively, so deleting these files. When you select file(s) and use the Delete key, you will be asked to confirm and reminded that this is a deletion rather than a (reversible) addition to the Recycle Bin.

126

Restoring files: Files that are contained in the Recycle Bin can be restored. Use the File — Open command for the Bin (either from Desktop or from Explorer). Select one or more files and click File — Restore.

Bin Options: If the Bin icon is visible on the Desktop, click with the right-hand mouse button and then on *Properties*. If you are using Explorer, click on the Bin icon and then on *Properties*. The *Properties* panel will have an additional tab labelled *General* if you start it from the Explorer view of one drive, but this can be ignored. The more important tab is labelled *Global*, followed by tabs for each hard drive or partition of a hard drive.

The Global tab has two option buttons labelled *Configure Drives Independently* (the default) and *Use One Setting for all Drives*. If you opt to use one setting for all drives, the remainder of the panel is available, and you can, if you want, opt not to use the Recycle Bin system at all by clicking on the selection box marked *Do not move files to the Recycle Bin. Remove files immediately on Deletion*. You can also opt to declare the maximum percentage of the hard drive(s) that can be used for the Recycle Bin, and you can tick a selection box to *Display Delete Confirmation Dialog*.

- If you use the default option of configuring drives independently, then you can use the tabs that are marked with the letters and names of your hard drives or partitions. Each panel will contain information on the drive size, space reserved for the Recycle Bin files, and the options to delete files directly, not using the Bin, and to declare how much space can be allocated, in that drive, to the Recycle bin.

Note: If disc space is low, opting to delete directly avoids wasting space with unwanted files, but you should ensure that you are using a good backup system.

Registry

Registry

General: The registry of Windows 95 is a database that contains a mass of information on the way that Windows and other software operates. This information is contained in two files that should be backed up at intervals. The registry files are checked and (if necessary) altered each time the computer is shut down; this is the reason for the delay between selecting *Shut Down* and getting the message that you can finally switch off.

Backup: The registry files are called SYSTEM.DAT and USER.DAT, and are located in the C:\WINDOWS folder. There is another pair of files, SYSTEM.DA0 and USER.DA0, which are duplicate backup files located in the same folder. You should, at intervals, make copies of the DAT files on to a floppy in case of any corruption of the Registry caused by hard drive failure. Though the copies will not be up to date, they will at least contain most of the Registry information that is needed to run the computer as it was configured at the time when the backups were made.

Editing: In normal circumstances it should never be necessary to alter the Registry files directly, only by way of options within programs (such as the *File Location* options in Word). You should not on any account alter Registry settings unless advised to do so in a book or a magazine article, and only if you back up the Registry files first. Careless alteration of the Registry files can severely restrict your use of Windows 95.

When it is necessary to edit the registry, you can either use a specialised editor (which will usually allow access only to some specific portions of the Registry) or the REGEDIT utility that is built into Windows 95. To start this editor, click on Start — Run and type REGEDIT (or click the arrowhead to see if this name is already present in the list). The *Editor*

128

panel shows an Explorer-type of display starting with *My Computer*, and with the six main portions of the Registry displayed with their names, all starting with HKEY. Each main title carries a [+] box that indicates that you can click on the box to expand the display, and most of the HKEY entries will expand to several levels, with information held only in the lowest levels. The database main sections are:

HKEY_CLASSES_ROOT   HKEY_CURRENT_USER

HKEY_LOCAL_MACHINE   HKEY_USERS

HKEY_CURRENT_CONFIG   HKEY_DYN_DATA

Of these, HKEY_CLASSES_ROOT contains information on association of data files with programs, and the sections that you are most likely to use are those that deal with current user, local machine and current configuration.

Restoration: If you do anything that scrambles the Registry information, you can return to the condition that the Registry had when you switched the computer on – this is more likely to be useful than restoring from a backup disc that might have been made some time ago. If you make a backup of the SYSTEM and USER data file before you use REGEDIT, you can use this backup to restore files in the eventuality of problems arising.

If you need to restore from the internal files, this is done by renaming the SYSTEM.DA0 and USER.DA0 files to the DAT extensions, but this **must** be done from MS-DOS rather than from Windows (since Windows may not be functioning). If you know how to use MS-DOS the procedure is fairly simple, but if you have never used MS-DOS you must follow the steps precisely. First, use Start — Shut Down, and select the *Restart the Computer in MS-DOS Mode* option. When the machine restarts, it will be running MS-DOS, not Windows, and you need to make certain that you are using the correct folder by typing CD C:\WINDOWS (press the RETURN or ENTER key). This assumes that your Windows files are in this folder – use whatever drive letter and folder is appropriate for your system.

Type each line as shown below, ending each line by pressing the RETURN or ENTER key. The spaces are important, as is the use of a zero in the names SYSTEM.DA0 and USER.DA0.

ATTRIB -H -R -S SYSTEM.DAT

ATTRIB -H -R -S SYSTEM.DA0

ATTRIB -H -R -S USER.DAT

ATTRIB -H -R -S USER.DA0

COPY SYSTEM.DA0 SYSTEM.DAT

COPY USER.DA0 USER.DAT

You should then switch off, wait, and restart the computer. When Windows 95 is started it will use the registry as it was before you made any alterations.

If you have make a backup of SYSTEM.DAT and USER.DAT to a floppy in the A: drive, you follow the method of restarting in MS-DOS mode, and then place the floppy in the A: drive. The MS-DOS instructions are then:

CD C:\WINDOWS

ATTRIB -H -R -S SYSTEM.DAT

ATTRIB -H -R -S USER.DAT

COPY A:*.DAT C:\WINDOWS

– remembering to press the RETURN or ENTER key. You can then restart the computer to run Windows 95.

Notes: From time to time, magazines issue instructions on

how to use the Registry for actions that are not available from Windows. You may feel that you are never likely to need these actions, but you should note them because if you ever need to edit the Registry you need all the help you can get.

- The REGEDIT program contains a command that allows you to export the registry files as text. This makes it possible to print the files and examine them at leisure rather than only when REGEDIT is running.

Right mouse button

General: The use of the right-hand mouse button was introduced in Windows 95, though some earlier programs featured non-standard actions induced by the right-hand mouse button. In Windows 95 programs, the right-hand mouse button always provides a short menu of useful actions, and the nature of the menu depends on the position of the cursor on the screen at the instant when the right-hand button is pressed. If a program (such as Word or Excel) is running, it may have its own menus for the right-hand button, and the descriptions below refer to its use on the Windows 95 desktop and Taskbar only.

Taskbar: Clicking with the right-hand button on any unused portion of the Taskbar (not on an icon) provides the menu of *Cascade*, *Tile Horizontally*, *Tile Vertically*, *Minimize All Windows* and *Properties*. The *Properties* menu item leads to the Taskbar and Start Menu properties panel, see the entries for these items. See also the entry for **cascade/tile** for a description of this action.

Desktop: Clicking with the right-hand button on any unused portion of the Desktop provides the menu of *Arrange Icons*, *Line Up Icons*, *Paste*, *Paste Shortcut*, *New* and *Properties*.

ScanDisk

The *Arrange Icon* options refer to the Desktop display (if you place several icons on the Desktop). The *New* item allows the main choice of *Folder* or *Shortcut*, with options for other objects, such as *Word Document*, that depend on what other software you use. The *Properties* item will display the set of tabs for *Display Properties*, see Display.

Recycle Bin: See the **Recycle Bin** entry for the menu that appears when you right-click over this icon.

My Computer: The right-click menu consists of *Explore* or *Open* (sometimes both), *Find*, *Create Shortcut*, *Rename* and *Properties*. This provides methods of placing a shortcut to *My Computer* in another folder, or of renaming it. The *Properties* item leads to the *System Properties* panel that you also find by double-clicking on *System* in *Control Panel*.

Program name: If you right-click on any of the program names in the Taskbar the menu consists of *Restore*, *Move*, *Size*, *Maximize*, *Minimize*, and *Close*.

File Name: If you right-click on a document file name, the menu consists of *Open*, *Send To*, *Cut*, *Copy*, *Create Shortcut*, *Delete*, *Rename* and *Properties*.

Notes: You can also drag a file or files using the right-hand mouse button. When you do this, a menu will appear when you drop the file(s) in another folder. The menu is normally *Move Here*, *Copy Here*, *Create Shortcut(s) Here* and *Cancel*, though if you drag to the Recycle Bin you will see only the *Move Here* and *Cancel* options.

ScanDisk

General: ScanDisk is a utility that will check the state of discs, hard or floppy, and report on their condition. ScanDisk can also ensure that any faulty areas of a hard drive are locked out of use so that they cannot result in loss of data. ScanDisk is automatically called up by other disc maintenance programs, notably the *Disk Defragmenter*.

Starting: Click Start — Programs — Accessories — System Tools — ScanDisk. The panel that appears asks you to select the drive you want to check. You can opt for either the *Standard check* (files and folders) or the *Thorough check* (files and folders, disc surface). A selection box can be ticked if you want to opt for *Automatically Fix Errors*.

Options: If you use the *Thorough check*, you can click the *Options* button to determine how ScanDisk will deal with your disc. The first options concern the areas of the disc that are scanned, with the options of *System and Data areas* (default), *System area only* and *Data Area only*. There is a selection box that can be ticked for *Do Not Perform Write Testing* and one labelled *Do not Repair Bad Sectors in Hidden and System files*. Normally, the disc surface is tested by reading the contents of each sector and writing them back to check that the write action does not cause errors. If this box is ticked, only the reading action will be checked – for all but a few exceptional cases you can leave this box un-ticked. The other box concerns the use of programs that expect to find a hidden file in a specific place and which refuse to run unless this file is found. Repairing a bad sector could result in shifting such a file, so that this provision is made for the (now unusual) case of programs that employ this action.

Advanced: The *Advanced* button can be clicked to reveal another set of options on a panel. The set headed *Display Summary* deals with the screen message that appears following ScanDisk, and you can opt for *Always*, *Never* or *Only on Error*. The *Lost File Fragments* section deals with parts of files that have no identification (usually deleted file fragments) and you can opt to *Free* them (so that the space is used by other files) or to *Convert to File* so that you can

Scraps

recover the data, if any. The conversion to a file option is a desperate way of trawling out the remnants of document files that have been deleted from the Recycle Bin.

The *Log File* section deals with the log file of text that reports the ScanDisk results. You can opt for *Replace Log* (old log is replaced by new version), *Append Log* (latest report is added to the end of the previous one) or *No Log*. The *Check Files For* section has selection boxes for *Invalid File Name* and for *Invalid Date/Time*, and you can check both. There is also a selection box that can be ticked for *Check Host Drive First*. This applies to a drive that uses DriveSpace (see **compression** entry), forcing ScanDisk to check the physical (host) drive before checking the compressed file. If you do not use DriveSpace you can ignore this box. The log file is called SCANDISK.LOG, and is a simple text (ASCII) file located in the C:\ root folder.

Notes: A thorough check on a hard drive can take some time. You will be reminded when you use the *My Computer* or *Explorer* properties panel with a hard drive selected, of how many days have elapsed since you carried out a check of your hard drive. You will also be reminded about backups and defragmentation.

....

Scraps

General: A scrap is a portion of text or graphics copied from a program to the Desktop. Such a scrap can be dragged into any other suitable document or into a program for editing. This avoids the need to save a selection to a file to be subsequently loaded or inserted into a document or program.

Creating: Make sure that you are working with a portion of the Desktop visible. Select a portion of text or graphics in a program or document. Drag this 'scrap' to the Desktop – it will appear as an icon, and the action is one of copying rather than moving. The icon will carry a name such as *Document Scrap*, along with an identifier such as the first few words of the scrap.

Using: The scrap can be dragged into any *compatible* document or program that supports this action. This does not necessarily mean that you can make use of the scrap. For example, if you create a scrap from a Word document and drag it into Notepad, you will not make much sense of the result. The scrap in this example has to be dragged into a Word (or WordPad) document to be readable. You cannot drag a scrap *from* Notepad.

Notes: Some programs, particularly graphics programs, do not allow scraps to be made, so that the dragging action will not move the selected object out of the Window area. If you hold down the *Shift* key as you drag a scrap to the Desktop, the action will be a *Move* action, so that the scrap disappears from the original document.

- -

Selecting

General: You can select a folder or file name so that you can carry out an action. More important, you can select more than one file or folder as a group so that an action such as copying or deleting will apply to all in the group.

Clicking: Click on a single file or folder in the My Computer or Explorer display to select that file or folder. You can hold down the Ctrl key and click on another name to add this to the selection (or you can click again to deselect one name). You can use the Edit — Select All menu item to select all the files in one folder. You can click one file, hold down the Shift key and then click another file to select all the files (inclusively) that lie between the two you have clicked. You

Send To

can also drag a selection window around a set of files (press the left-hand mouse button down over one file and drag to another).

MS-DOS text selection: If you have opened a document using an MS-DOS program, you may not be able to use mouse selection. If you cannot use the mouse to drag over text, click Edit — Mark and then click at the start of the text you want to select. Hold down the Shift key, and click on the end of the text block. You can then use the Edit — Copy menu action to put the text on the Clipboard, from which it can be pasted into any other program that is editing a document, MS-DOS or Windows.

Notes: See the **MS-DOS** entry for the actions of *Quick Edit* and *Fast Paste* applied to documents opened under MS-DOS.

Send To

General: The *Send To* action is a file action that is available from My Computer or Explorer, or from the right-hand mouse button menu when a file name is selected. The default destination for the *Send To* action is a floppy drive, but you can add other destinations in a folder called *Send To*.

Using: Select the file you want to use, click with the right-hand mouse button, and then on the *Sent To* item. Click on the destination that you want to use.

Destination: Using *My Computer* or *Explorer*, click on the C:\WINDOWS\Send To folder. Use the File — New menu item and select *Shortcut*. You will see the Shortcut Wizard appear and you can type a destination or click the *Browse* button to find a suitable destination

Notes: Remember that when you use a shortcut to a printer, this will start up a suitable program when you use *Send To*.

For example, if you use *Send To* (aimed at the printer) on a DOC file, Word will be started, the document loaded in, and the Print action of Word used.

....

Shortcuts

General: A shortcut is a small file, usually about 100 bytes, which is a form of path-pointer to a program or document file or to a device such as a floppy disc drive or printer. The advantage of using shortcuts is that they can be placed in any folder, avoiding the need to have to remember a path to a destination. More than one shortcut can be used referring to one destination.

Creating: By far the simplest method is to use the Wizard, starting from an Explorer or My Computer display. Click on the folder in which you want to place the shortcut. Click File — New and then *Shortcut*. Either type the name of the object or folder, or use *Browse* to find the object or folder, and click for the next step of the Wizard. Another method that is particularly useful for a file is to click on the name, hold down the Ctrl and Shift keys, then drag the filename to the destination folder where you want the shortcut established.

Deleting: Select the shortcut and press the Delete key. Deleting a shortcut does not delete the object or program to which it is a shortcut.

Copying: Use an Explorer or My Computer view, click the shortcut, and then Edit — Copy. Open the folder that is to receive the Shortcut and click Edit — Paste.

Settings: Click the shortcut using the right-hand mouse button, and then click the *Properties* item on the menu. The *General* panel that appears contains information about the Shortcut file, and clicking the *Shortcut* tab will show information that is more useful to you, particularly the

Sound Recorder

Target, Start In, Shortcut keys, and *Run* lines. The *Target* line shows the path to the file or object that the shortcut leads to, and the *Start In* line will often show the same folder, but can show a folder that is used to start a program. The *Shortcut key* (or hot key) line will by default show *None*, but you can click in this line and then press down keys that you will use to start the shortcut. You must include the Ctrl or Alt key (or both) and a letter key. Because the shortcut key line will not accept key combinations that are used in Windows you may find that the combination is not exactly as you typed (you might press Ctrl-N and get Ctrl-Alt-N).

Notes: Excessive use of shortcuts can seriously reduce your hard drive space, because the hard drive is organised so that it uses a minimum size (the cluster size) of file. For example, depending on the size of your drive, a 100-byte file may take up a 16 Kbyte space.

- -

Sound Recorder

General: The Sound Recorder can be used if you have a sound card and a suitable microphone, CD player, tape cassette player, or other sound source, plugged into it. You can then create sound 'objects' represented by icons for WAV files that can be pasted into documents. Double-clicking on a sound object icon will play the sound. You need some knowledge of digital sound recording principles to get the best out of Sound Recorder. You will probably need a considerable amount of trial and error to obtain satisfactory results with a microphone.

Starting: Click Start — Programs — Accessories — Multimedia — Sound Recorder, or double-click the file SNDREC32.EXE in an Explorer display. You can place a shortcut to this file in any folder or on the Desktop if you want faster access.

Creating a sound object: Make sure that your microphone, preferably a good moving-coil type, is plugged into the sound card. Start *Sound Recorder* and click the File — New item. Click the *Start* button to begin recording and the *Stop* button when you have finished. Use File — Save As to save the sound as a file. Remember that a fairly short speech can require a fairly large amount of memory space unless you opt for telephone-quality. If you use a CD player or cassette-player as your sound source you will need to opt for higher quality and use much more disc space.

Playing a sound: You can replay a sound using either *Sound Recorder* or **Media Player** (see entry). To replay from *Sound Recorder*, click File — Open and click the name of a sound file you have recorded. Click the *Play* button to start, and the *Stop* button to stop. You can also use the 'fast wind' controls to move to the start or the end of a sound recording.

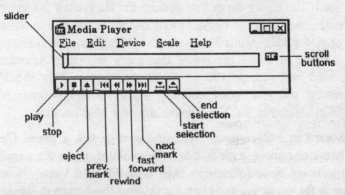

Audio Properties: Click the *Sound Recorder* Edit — Audio Properties menu item to see the Panel which allows you to control volume and quality separately from the *Options* tab. The *Audio Properties* panel is in two parts, *Recording* and *Replaying*, and for each there is a slider volume control. As a rough guide, the recording volume control needs to be set *High* for a microphone input and *Low* for inputs from CD

Sound Recorder

players or cassette tape players. You can also pick the quality level from this panel (see later for explanation). The preferred device that appears will be the sound card that is installed on your computer. You should ensure that the box marked *Show Volume Control on the Taskbar* is ticked – see the entry for **Volume Control.**

Options: With the *Sound Recorder* panel displayed, click File — Properties. The panel that appears allows you to control recording quality and the system that is used to convert sound into digital signals. On this panel, a section headed *Format Conversion* opens up your options. You have the choice of *Recording Formats, Playback Formats* and *All Formats*, and whichever you select can be modified by clicking on the *Convert Now* button. The options are detailed in the following sections. Each format can be described in terms of quality or by a formal name for the system that is used. The higher the quality you opt for, the greater the use of disc space, and the figure to look out for is the rate in terms of KB/s. This means Kilobytes per second, and, for example, a figure of 100 KB/s means that every second of recorded sound will require 100 Kbyte of disc space. This should remind you that sound recording requires a large amount of precious disc space. See also the entry for **Multimedia.**

Sound in a document: You can insert or link a sound file into a document, such as a text file in Word. Open the sound file using *Sound Recorder*, and click Edit — Copy. Now open the document and click the place in the document where you want the sound icon to be put. Click Edit — Paste. If you want to link the sound file, use the Edit — Paste Special option and select *Paste Link*. If there is no *Paste Special* option in the *File* menu, the program that holds the document does not support linking and only embedding can be used. An embedded sound can make a document length very much greater than you would expect from the amount of text that it contains.

Recording/Playback Formats: When you click the *Convert Now* button you will see another panel open with displays for *Name*, *Format* and *Attributes*, and buttons marked *Save As* and *Remove*. The range of name (click the arrowhead) is *Unnamed*, *CD quality*, *Radio quality* and *Telephone quality*. This form of naming makes it easier to select the quality level that you need, and you can read the *Attributes* panel to see what *Format* and combination of *Attributes* are used. If you alter the *Format* or the *Attributes*, the name will change to *Untitled*, allowing you to create a quality level for your own use. The fixed names are:

Telephone quality	11K	8-bit mono	11 KB/s
Radio quality	22K	8-bit mono	22 KB/s
CD quality	44K	16-bit stereo	172 KB/s

with the figures showing, in order, the sampling rate, number of bits per sample, and number of kilobytes per second. The sampling rate is the number of samples of the sound wave per second used to convert the wave into a set of numbers for digital recording.

If you want to make a scheme of your own you can choose from the formats and attributes that are on offer – these may depend on which sound card you are using. A typical list is *CCITT A-Law*, *CCITT u-Law*, *IMA ADPCM*, *Microsoft ADPCM* and *PCM* (the usual default). Your own scheme can be named and saved using the *Save As* button.

All Formats: When you use the *All Formats* option in the main panel and click the *Convert Now* button you will see the usual list of named schemes, but you have a wider choice for Untitled, typically with some very tightly compressed formats such as *DSP Group True Speech*. A typical set is:

Sound Recorder

CCITT-A Law	8 kHz, 8 bit, mono	8KB/s
CCITT-u Law	8 kHz, 8 bit, mono	8KB/s
DSP True Speech	8 kHz, 1 bit, mono	1 KB/s
GSM 6.10	8 kHz, mono	2 KB/s
IMA ADPCM	8 kHz, 4-bit, mono	4 KB/s
Microsoft ADPCM	8 kHz, 4 bit, mono	4 KB/s
PCM	8 kHz, 8 bit, mono	8 KB/s

Editing sounds: When you have made a sound recording, you can edit it as if it were on a tape. You can delete a part of the sound file by moving the *Recorder* position indicator (slider) to the point where you want to start cutting. Now click Edit — Delete After Current Position to delete all that follows, or Edit — Delete Before Current Position to delete all that comes earlier in the file.

If the *Sound Recorder* display shows a green line (to indicate that the file uses an uncompressed format) you can change the playback speed by using Effects — Increase Speed or Effects — Decrease Speed. Each change is up by 100% (doubled) or down by 50% (halved). The volume of an uncompressed file can also be changed in 25% increments by using the *Effects* menu. Uncompressed files can also be played in reverse using Effects — Reverse and then clicking the *Play* button, and an echo can be added using Effects — Add Echo.

- Any changes that you have made to a sound file which has not been saved can be cancelled by using File — Revert. Once you save a file the changes are fixed.

Start button

You can use the *Edit* menu items of *Insert File* and *Mix with File* (which also exist in *Paste* versions) to replace part of an existing sound file with another sound file (*Insert*) or to mix the files so that you hear the sound of both. This is easier if you have had some experience of conventional sound mixing, and the actions are possible only if the sound files are uncompressed.

Notes: If you need to keep a document size down, you can link in the sound objects. Making an ASCII version of a document will cut out all sound objects.

- -

Start button

General: The Start button is the starting point for most of the Windows 95 actions. Many of these actions have already been described under other headings, so that most of the following is a summary only of the Start button actions.

Run: The *Run* item is used when you need to run a program that is not normally available. It can be used for REGEDIT (see the entry for **Registry**), for example, and for running setup programs from a floppy. The arrowhead on the *Run* line can be clicked to select commands that have been used in the past. You should not use *Run* unless you are directed to, because installing modern programs should be done by using the Control Panel *Add/Remove Programs* item.

- Run can, however, be used to open shared folders over a network.

Help: The Help item will start the main Windows 95 Help system, allowing you to look up help topics in the index, or the search for help.

Start button

Find: The Find item will start the Find action which is available also from Explorer.

Settings: This item brings up a sub-menu of Control Panel, Printers and Taskbar. These settings can be made also from Explorer. Remember that if Explorer (or the Explorer window of My Computer) is running when you shut down the computer, it will automatically start again when you switch on.

Documents: This menu item will reveal all the most-recently edited document names, in the form of shortcuts placed in a *Documents* folder. You can load a document into the program that created it, and edit the document, by clicking on the document name in this list. You can use Start — Settings — Taskbar to see a *Clear* button which can be clicked to remove all *Document* shortcuts. You should clear out the *Document* list at intervals, because a large number of shortcuts can take up a disproportionate amount of space on your hard drive.

Programs: This item leads to the main folder list, starting with Accessories and containing *MS-DOS Prompt* and *Windows Explorer*. You can add other sets using Explorer.

Adding/removing programs: When Windows 95 was installed on your computer, a set of programs was placed into the Start menu, and programs that you have installed since will also have been added. You may want to place other programs into the Start set, however. The simplest method is to open the *Start Menu* folder of C:\WINDOWS and open whichever subfolder you want to use (such as *Programs*, *Accessories*, etc.). You can then create a shortcut to the program you want in that subfolder. You can remove programs from the Start menu by deleting the corresponding shortcut in its subfolder.

The more formal method is to click Start — Settings — Taskbar and click the *Start Menu Programs* tab. You can opt to *Add* or *Remove* a program, and a Wizard will then guide you through the process. When you opt to *Add*, you can click a *Browse* button to assist you in finding the path to the program you want. The *Advanced* button of this set simply leads to an Explorer type of display so that you can work with the folders directly rather than through the Wizard.

- Any program file shortcuts that you place into the *Startup* subfolder will run when you start Windows, so that you can have all of your favourite programs running when you start. You can click the shortcut name with the right-hand mouse button and click the *Properties* item to determine whether you want to be able to use a shortcut key combination, or what size of window to use when the program is started.

- You can add new sub-folders to the Start Menu set by using Explorer and creating a new folder in the usual way.

- You do not need to put Explorer in the Startup menu – it will restart automatically if it was running when you switched down Windows 95.

Shut Down: You use this option to shut down the computer in an orderly way, so that the **Registry** (see entry) can be modified to accommodate any changes that you have made. You should not simply switch off. Click the *Shut Down* option and select which option you want, usually *Shut Down* (options of *Restart* and *Restart in MS-DOS Mode*). You can use the No button if you change your mind at this point. While the Registry is being updated you will see a screen message asking you to wait, and you should not switch off until you see a message in red telling you that it is now safe to do so. If you switch off prematurely you risk losing data.

Startup disc, creating

Notes: The Start menu operates by using shortcuts, see the entry for **Shortcuts**.

. . . .

Startup disc, creating

General: A startup disc is a floppy that allows your computer to be started in the event of a failure of the hard drive or corruption of essential system files. If such a failure occurs, the startup disc can be placed in the floppy drive and the machine can then be started running MS-DOS (not Windows). The disc then contains sufficient software to carry out diagnostic tests and to allow Windows 95 to be re-installed if necessary. Some knowledge of MS-DOS and the Windows system is needed for this type of work, but you should always keep at least one startup disc at hand in case of emergency.

Preparation: Start *Control Panel* from *Explorer* or from Start — Settings. Double-click on *Add/Remove* Programs and then on the tab marked *Startup Disc*. Click the *Create Disc* button. You will be asked to insert the Windows 95 CD-ROM or first floppy into the appropriate drive. After some files have been read, you will be asked to insert a blank 1.4 Mbyte floppy disc into the A:\ drive and reminded that any data on the disc will be deleted. Files are then (slowly) copied to the floppy. Apart from the thermometer display of progress, you will not see any notice to tell you that the process is complete. All but 75 Kbyte of the floppy will be used.

Using: If the computer refuses to start normally from the hard drive, switch off and allow a few minutes. Insert the startup disc in the A:\ drive and switch on again. This time the computer will start from the floppy files, running MS-DOS. You can then run ScanDisk (from the floppy) to check your hard drive, and you can also run REGEDIT to check the

Windows Registry files for corruption. Advanced (and experienced) users can run the DEBUG program to read drive and memory content.

Notes: A Startup disc is no substitute for using a good backup system. As well as keeping a Startup disc you should keep floppy copies of the registry files and any data files that you could not otherwise replace in the event of failure of a hard drive.

StartUp folder

General: The Startup folder contains shortcuts to programs, and when Windows 95 is started, these programs will be loaded and run. You can determine for each program whether it will run full-screen, in its default window size, or minimised. This allows you to start Windows with all your favourite programs ready to use. Note that you do not need to have Explorer (or the Explorer format of My Computer) in this set because these programs will start automatically if they have been in use when the computer was closed down.

You can also use Explorer to create new folders (using File — New) in any part of the Start Menu. You can, for example, click the Programs folder and create new folders called Communications, Data, Drawing, Financial Etc., so that your Programs list contains these new titles, and you can then place program shortcuts into these folders.

Add/Remove programs: By far the simplest way, when you have some experience with Explorer, is to display the C:\WINDOWS\Start Menu\Programs\Startup folder. You can then create shortcuts in this folder for the programs you want, and you can also delete shortcuts to programs that you no longer need to be loaded ready for you.

The other method is to use Start — Settings — Taskbar, and

Status bar

click the *Start Menu Programs* button. You can opt to *Add* or *Remove* programs and the Wizard will then guide you to browse for the program you want to add or find the program you want to remove. The Advanced button can be clicked to allow you to use Explorer to alter files and folders and read the Properties of files and shortcuts to files.

Notes: You do not need to place Explorer or My Computer in the Startup menu. If either or both of these programs is running when you switch off it will resume when you re-start the computer.

Status bar

General: The status bar of a Windows 95 program is located at the bottom of the window, and carries information on your current folder or file selection. For example the status bar of Explorer shows the size of a selected file, the size of a selected folder, and the free space on a selected hard drive or floppy disc.

Switching: You can usually switch the status bar display on or off. For example, when you are using Explorer, you can click View — Status Bar to switch the bar on (tick appears in menu) or off.

Notes: The information that appears in a Status Bar is often useful, so that you should preferably opt to make this item visible.

System files

General: The system files of Windows 95 and MS-DOS are programs that are essential to the running of the operating system. System files must not be deleted, and in some cases should not even be moved, so that Windows 95 allows the names of system files to be concealed in an Explorer display.

Concealing: From Explorer, click View — Options to see the *View* tab. The default setting is *Show All Files*, but you can alter this by clicking *Hide files of these types*. The types that will be concealed are files that carry the extensions DLL, SYS, VXD, 386 and DRV.

Notes: The majority of system files are DLL (dynamic link library) types, and your system may not use some of them. You can use the File — Properties item of Explorer to find out what the file is used for, selecting the *Version* tab, and clicking *Product Name*. If the *Product Name* is Windows 95, it is fairly certain that you might cause problems by deleting such a file. If the *Product Name* shows a program that you have deleted or which you have not installed, you might be able to delete the file. Many DLL files are shared, however, so that you cannot be certain whether a file is used or not. If you delete a DLL file, keep it on the Recycle Bin or on a floppy until you are quite certain you don't need it. Some files may be used only at infrequent intervals, such as files belonging to *ScanDisk* or *Disk Defragmenter*, so that you would not know that you had deleted an important DLL file until you tried to use a program that required it.

Notes: One problem that can arise is that installing an old program may cause a modern DLL file to be replaced by an older version that uses the same name. You may be able to reinstate the modern version if you know where to find a copy.

- -

Taskbar

General: The Windows 95 Taskbar is the strip at the foot of the screen which displays the Start button along with buttons for any programs that are running. The right-hand corner of the Taskbar can also display icons, such as the loudspeaker

Taskbar

(for *Volume Control*), other programs, and the time.

Position: The Taskbar can be dragged to the top or either side of the screen. When it is dragged to the side, most of the titles will be cut short, but you can place the cursor on the edge of the bar, so that the double-arrow cursor appears, and then drag out the width of the Taskbar. For most purposes, the default position is better.

Options: Click Start — Settings — Taskbar. The four selection boxes on the Taskbar Options panel are marked *Always on Top*, *Auto Hide*, *Show Small Icons in Start Menu*, and *Show Clock*. The *Always on Top* item should be ticked, as it ensures that the Taskbar can always be seen over a maximised window. You can use *Auto Hide* if you like to run programs maximised, and do not want to lose part of the window space to the Taskbar. If you use this option, you will see the Taskbar appear when you move the mouse pointer to the bottom of the screen and hold it there. The *Show Small Icons* option can be clicked if you feel that the icon size in the Start menu looks too large on a 640 × 480 display – on 800 × 600 or higher the problem is usually to see icons without using a magnifying glass. Click the *Show Clock* icon for a display of time at the bottom right-hand corner of the Taskbar. Placing the cursor on this time display will bring up a date display.

Programs: When a program name appears on the Taskbar (in minimised form) you can click with the left-hand mouse button to restore the program to the active window, or you can click with the right-hand mouse button to close the program. The Alt-Tab key method of switching from one program to another (as used on Windows 3.1) can be used also on Windows 95, and does not require the Taskbar to be visible.

- You can minimise all open windows by clicking a blank

place on the Taskbar using the right-hand mouse button and selecting *Minimize All Windows*. If you then click again on a blank portion of the Taskbar, you will find that the menu includes *Undo Minimize All*, allowing you to restore all windows.

- When the printer is in use with spooling (the default) a printer icon will appear on the right hand side of the default Taskbar. Double-click this icon to see the print queue display.

Notes: If you keep a large number of programs running, the Taskbar descriptions will be very brief.

....

Text

General: The text that appear in Windows 95, as distinct from text in editing or word-processing programs, can be copied and changes to fonts can be made. Even the Help screens allow a choice of fonts.

Copying text: Select the text (in a dialogue box or a Help box) that you want to copy and then click on the selected text with the right-hand mouse button. Click the *Copy* commands in the menu. Switch to a text editor or word processor and use the *Paste* action to complete the copying. Text can also be copied from one dialogue box to another, using the *Paste* command (if available) from the right-hand mouse button menu.

Adding text: You can add text as an annotation to a Help item, see the entry for **Help**.

Font and size: Start Control Panel from Explorer or from Start — Settings. Double-click on *Display*, and on the *Appearance* tab. Click *Custom* to change the font size for displays of 800 × 600 or higher. For such displays, you can

ToolTips

also opt to make the screen display match actual size. Hold a ruler, calibrated in inches, against the image of a ruler on the panel, and drag the end of the screen ruler so that it exactly matches the size of the real ruler. The drawback of this is that some fonts may then appear much too small for easy reading on a 14″ screen. Note that these changes do **not** apply if you are using the default 640 × 480 screen resolution.

- See the entry for **Desktop** for changing fonts and sizes of text in standard window displays. See the **Help** entry for changing Help fonts.

Notes: If you make changes to the Desktop appearance, save your Desktop setup as a file so that you can restore it if you subsequently make other changes that you regret.

ToolTips

General: ToolTips are the short messages that appear under the mouse pointer when you hold the pointer over an icon. The use of ToolTips can be switched on or off in some programs, though not in Windows itself, and the appearance of the tips can be changed.

Appearance: Start Control Panel from Explorer or from Start — Settings and double-click Display. Select the *Appearance* tab, and click the arrowhead on the *Item* line. Scroll down to the last item which is ToolTips. You can then change the colour of background used for ToolTips, and the font type, size and colour of the printing in a ToolTip.

Notes: If a program allows you to switch ToolTips on or off you should preferably work with ToolTips on. Some programs will not permit the use of ToolTips.

Volume Control

General: The Volume Control is a display of a set of slider controls for use with a sound card when you are using Multimedia. The easiest way of using the Volume Control is to keep it as an icon on the Taskbar. Double-clicking this icon will bring up the volume control display.

Place on Taskbar: Start Control Panel from Explorer or from Start — Settings, and double-click *Multimedia*. On the first tab, labelled *Audio*, click the selection box marked *Show Volume Control on Taskbar* so that the box is ticked.

Running: If the volume control icon (a loudspeaker shape) appears on the Taskbar at the right hand side, double-click on it. If you are not using the Volume Control on the Taskbar, click Start — Programs — Accessories — Multimedia — Volume Control.

Using: The Volume Control displays slider controls for all the inputs and outputs that your sound card can deal with. A typical set is *Volume Control*, *Wave*, *MIDI*, *CD*, *Line in*, *Microphone* and *PC Speaker*. The *Volume Control* slider is a master control, and the settings of the others should be organised so that they all give about the same signal level, in or out, for a given setting of the master *Volume Control* slider. You can mute any of the sources, and if you are using the Volume Control for recording, you should mute all inputs except the one you want to use. Similarly, on replay, you should mute all outputs except the one you intend to use, which is likely to be *CD*. You can also change balance for stereo signals for each channel.

Options: The *Advanced* button will appear when you use Options — Advanced Controls. Clicking this button allows you to adjust *Bass* and *Treble* response. A *Bass* response setting higher than normal can be used partially to compensate for the deficiencies of small loudspeakers

What's This?

Notes: If you often play audio CDs through the system you should place the Volume Control on the Taskbar.

What's This?

General: The *What's This* icon of a question mark is useful for getting more detailed information on portions of a panel, particularly if you want to know how to fill in a form.

Icon: When the question-mark icon appears on the right hand of the title bar of a window, or when the *Help* menu contains a *What's This* item, you can use this type of *Help*.

Method: Click on the icon or on the menu item. A question mark icon will appear on the pointer, and you can move the pointer to the part of the window that puzzles you and click there. After a short wait, a *Help* item will appear which gives specific guidance on that item.

Notes: *What's This* may be brief, but it allows you to query each part of an elaborate panel before you enter any information.

Window

General: A window can be maximised, filling the screen, or minimised, reduced to an icon on the Taskbar. Between these extremes, you can resize most windows by dragging their edges or corners, though a few, like Windows Calculator, cannot be resized. You can opt for using a specified window size when a program is started by way of a shortcut, see the entry for **Shortcuts**. Closing a window is equivalent to quitting a program.

Icons: Each window will normally contain a set of three icons at the top right hand corner of the window, and a

Window

Microsoft or other icon (menu icon) at the top left hand corner. The set of three icons will contain the cross icon which is used to close the window, and two of the three possible size icons of *minimise, normal* and *maximise*. The minimise icon will reduce the window to an icon and name on the Taskbar. The maximise icon will cause the window to take up all the useable screen area. The normal icon can be clicked to make the window resume the size that it had when last resized (not minimised nor maximised).

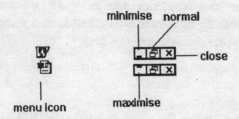

Menus: Clicking the Microsoft or other icon at the top left-hand corner of a window will bring up a menu of *Restore, Move, Size, Minimise, Maximise* and *Close*. Double-clicking the icon will close the window – this is an alternative to clicking on the cross icon.

Size: Drag any edge or corner of a window to alter the window size. Dragging a corner is preferable because it allows you to change both width and depth in one action. A few windows, such as Calculator, cannot be resized because they contain items, such as buttons, whose size is fixed.

Closing program: A program is closed when its window is closed, but you may prefer to close a program by using the *Exit* option in its *File* menu, or the equivalent. A few programs (such as communications programs) will not necessarily terminate when their window is closed.

Starting window size: Using Explorer, click on a shortcut to

WordPad

a program file and then on File — Properties. Click on the tab labelled *Shortcut*, and then click the arrowhead on the *Run* space. This offers the choice of *Normal Window*, *Maximized* or *Minimized*. Click your choice and then on the *OK* button.

Notes: The left-hand top corner icon can be clicked with either left or right-hand mouse button. The right-hand top corner icons can be clicked only with the left-hand mouse button.

- Remember that you can *Minimize All Windows* by clicking with the right-hand mouse button on a vacant part of the Taskbar and selecting this item.

WordPad

General: WordPad is the word processor for Windows 95 that replaces the older *Write* used in Windows 3.1. The advantage of using WordPad is that its files are identical to those of Word 7, and the older Write files can be read. Some facilities of *Write* have not been retained, such as *Header and Footer* text, or a line-spacing option. For some purposes, such as preparation of books or articles, this makes WordPad less satisfactory than the older version, so that its main use is for reading, editing, or creating documents that are too long for Notepad. If you use Word, then there is little point in retaining WordPad on the hard drive.

Opening: Start WordPad from Start — Programs — Accessories, assuming that the program has been placed in this menu when Windows 95 was installed. You can make a shortcut to WordPad in any part of the Start menu, or in any other folder, as you find convenient.

Screen: WordPad uses a screen appearance that is similar to Word 7, with a set of action icons on a *Toolbar*, font details

WordPad

on a *Formatting bar*, a *Ruler* and a *Status bar*. The *Toolbar*,
Format bar, *Ruler* and *Status bar* can all be turned on or off
using the *View* menu.

Page Setup: Before a document is printed (and preferably
before it is typed) use File — Page Setup to define the paper
size and other details. The size box contains the selection of
paper and envelope sizes as follows:

A4	210 × 297 mm	Executive	7¼ × 9½ inch
Legal	8½ × 14 inch	Letter	8½ × 11 inch
#10 envelope	4⅛ × 9 ½	C5 envelope	162 × 229 mm
DL envelope	110 × 220 mm	Monarch envelope	3⅞ × 7½ inch

You can also opt for Portrait (long side vertical) or
Landscape (long side horizontal) paper orientation, and you
can set the margins. The units of measurement are as defined
in *Options*, see later. The default margins are probably wider
than you might wish, 31.25 mm at left and right and 25.4 mm
(1 inch) at top and bottom.

Options: Click View — Options for the option panel of six
tabs labelled as *Options*, *Text*, *Rich Text*, *Word 6*, *Write* and
Embedded. The *Options* tab can be clicked to allow you a
choice of four measurement units, inches, centimetres, points
or picas. The point is a unit of ¹/₇₂ inch, and a pica is 12
points. The other five tabs deal with the different forms of
text files that WordPad can read, and in each panel you will
find options for *Word Wrap* and for *Toolbars*. The *Word
Wrap* options are *No wrap*, *Wrap to Window* and *Wrap to
Ruler*, and the *Toolbars* options are *Toolbar*, *Format Bar*,
Ruler and *Status Bar*. This allows you to determine how
Wordpad will look when you are importing and editing these

WordPad

files. You might, for example, want to use plain text with no word wrap and all Toolbars off, but use Word-6 files with word wrap to *Ruler* and with all *Toolbars* on.

Formatting: The WordPad Format menu allows four choices, *Font*, *Bullet type*, *Paragraph* and *Tabs*. The *Font* choice covers all of the fonts that have been installed into your computer, but you should use only the TrueType fonts if you want to print your work. Bullets are large dots used to make a paragraph or line more prominent, and you can use the *Bullet type* item on the menu to convert an ordinary paragraph into one that starts with a bullet and is indented. There is no choice of bullet characters. The *Bullet* icon on the Toolbar is an alternative to the use of the menu, and you can remove a bullet by clicking again either on the icon or on the menu item.

The *Paragraph* menu item provides a panel on which you can select indentation for a paragraph in terms of *Left*, *Right* and *First Line*. You can indent a whole paragraph or have the first line with a larger indent or with a zero or smaller indent (a hanging indent). You can also choose the alignment for the paragraph as *Left*, *Center* or *Right*, but not for full alignment, which is much more desirable in printed documents.

The *Tabs* item allows you to specify a tab position by typing in the distance from the left margin and clicking on the *Set* button (or on the *Clear* button to clear a tab at that position). The faster alternative is to click on the ruler line so that a dotted vertical line appears. This can be dragged to wherever you want to set a tab, and such tabs can be removed by dragging them off the *Ruler* line. If you do not set any tabs, a set of default tabs, which cannot be removed, at ½ inch spacings will be used. These default tabs are indicated by small dots under the *Ruler*; the tabs that you set for yourself are indicates by larger square dots. When you set a tab by using the menu or the *Ruler* line, the default tabs to the left of your tab setting will be ignored, but the default tabs will continue to be used to the right of the last tab that you set for yourself. The menu action allows you to remove all of the tabs that you have set, using a *Clear All* button.

Insertions: You can use the Insert menu to insert *Date and Time* or *Object*. *Clicking Date and Time* will insert the current information into your WordPad document at the position of the cursor, and you can select from six date formats and two time formats. These are:

| 04/07/96 | 4/7/96 | 040796 | 04 July 1996 |

| 4 July 1996 | 09:49:43 | 9:49:43 |

The first time format uses a 24-hour clock, the second uses PM to show times later than noon.

Object insertion covers the insertion of other text files, drawings and sounds, and the following description concentrates on insertion of a graphic to serve as an example. When you click on *Object* you will see a panel that allows you to choose *Create New* or *Create from File*. The *Create from New* item will allow you to run a program, in this example a Graphics program, to create the object so that it can be inserted. Using the *Create from File* option allows you to browse for a suitable graphics document file to use.

When you have found a file, you can click the box marked *Link* to link the file, or leave the box unticked to embed the file. When you opt to create a file, the program that you choose opens and you can make your drawing, but you should not use the File menu to close the file, because the File menu that you see is likely to be that of WordPad. When you use the *Create* option, you return to WordPad by clicking outside the file area, and the drawing or other object is embedded, not linked. If you want to link files, you have to create the file separately and save it before using WordPad to insert the object.

When an object is linked or embedded, you can use Edit — Properties from WordPad to see information about the object. For an embedded object, such as would be created using *Create from New*, the *Edit* panel has two tabs marked *General* and *View*. The *General* panel shows the *Type*, *Size* and *Location* of the object, with a button marked *Convert* that is available if the object can be converted to another format. If, as is more usual, the object cannot be converted, the button is greyed out. The *View* panel has options *Display as Editable Information* and *Display as Icon*, with a button marked *Change Icon* that can be used if you opt for display as an icon. Icon display is more usual for sound objects, and the sound will be heard when you double-click the icon. For a graphics file, double-clicking the icon produces a view of the drawing. In this panel, there is also a *Scale* display, allowing you to change the percentage scaling for objects that allow this action. You can also opt for scaling *Relative to Original Size* if the object can be scaled.

There is a third tab for linked objects. This shows the file to which the links are attached, and a button marked *Change Source* which you can press to link in a different file. An *Update* section has options of *Automatically* (the default) or *Manually*, and there are buttons *for Open Source*, *Update Now* and *Break Links*. If the link has been updated previously, the *Last Update* information will appear.

- The *Edit* menu also contains a *Links* item when a linked image is selected, allowing you the same actions as are present in the third *Properties* tab.

The *Edit* menu also has another reference to an embedded or linked object. The item names the object, such as *Bitmap Image Object* or *Linked Bitmap Image Object*. In either case, selecting this item will provide the options of *Edit* or *Open*. For a linked object, either will start a graphics editor (Paint for a bitmap image) running, but for an embedded object, *Edit* will allow editing in the document and *Open* will start the creating program running. To leave an *Edit*, click outside the object space, but to leave the *Open* action you need to quit the program, such as Paint, from a File — Exit and Return to Document command.

Toolbar: The Toolbar of WordPad contains icons for *New*, *Open*, *Save*, *Print*, *Print Preview*, *Find*, *Cut*, *Copy*, *Paste*, *Undo* and *Time/Date insertion*. These provide faster alternatives for actions that are also catered for in the menus. You can switch the Toolbar off by using the *View* menu.

Send: The File — Send item will send a copy of the WordPad document by electronic mail, assuming that you have installed Microsoft Exchange. When you click on the *Send* item, the file is saved, and a Wizard takes over.

Notes: When you double-click on a text file, Notepad will automatically be used (see entry for **association**) but if the file is too large for Notepad to handle you will be offered the option of using WordPad.